MAKIN A MACKEM

Julie Carter

By the Same Author

Running the Red Line

"In this ambitious, moving and tender book, Julie Carter examines how long-distance running can give life meaning, and how life itself makes running meaningful. The body and what we inherit, the damage that familial violence can cause and an intimate knowledge of the landscape and the art of running weave together in this unforgettable and inspiring work."

Dr Kim Moore, Poet and Essayist, Lecturer in
Creative Writing Manchester Metropolitan University.

"A great read and I love the interweaving of reflections, past and present, during the run which Julie takes us along.

Being an endurance runner myself I know how much time we spend in our own heads, making sense of the world and this is a real, gritty account of how running can help us to rationalise and make sense of happenings, even ones that occurred many years earlier.

Also, a great example of how anyone can take up the sport and achieve extraordinary things. Every runner has their own story about why they do it and this one is enthralling."

Alyson Dixon, Olympic Marathon Runner from Sunderland.

"A fascinating and moving account which meanders between pilgrimage and memoir and gives a wonderful insight into the nature of inheritance."

Dr Michael Crawley, author of
'*Out of Thin Air: Running Wisdom and Magic from Above the Clouds in Ethiopia*',
Assistant Professor in Social Anthropology Durham University.

"The unfolding of two journeys; one an endurance run through the physical landscapes of Northern England; the other an exploration of the emotional landscapes of an astounding life. This is a story of strength: the strength to escape the trauma of an abused and abusive working-class childhood; the strength to turn tenuous dreams into rewarding realities; the strength to keep running, keep hoping and keep seeking a sense connection. Julie's life is a journey which embodies hope, it's an inspiration to share it through these pages."

Geoff Cox, Author, Filmmaker, Runner and Mackem.

"Makin a Mackem reveals what it means for a single body to transcend. Contouring through landscapes of past and present, through adversity, class, and illness, Julie's story illustrates the meaning of perseverance and why it matters."

Dr Karen Lloyd, Author and Writer in Residence
with Lancaster University's Future Places Centre.

"This is the story of a woman, the place and the people she came from and how she learned to "run into her own skin". It traces the long shadow cast by experiences of trauma as a child and reveals how these can follow and compromise a person into adulthood. It is utterly candid, compelling, poetic and staggeringly good. She invites us to join her on an evocative and breath-taking journey across the elements of the landscape of her life past and present. This raw, wise, humorous and touching memoir is an inspirational and compelling read for any human being engaged in the often troubling and difficult endeavour of growing into the history of their own life."

Maggie Gregson, Professor of Vocational Education Sunderland University.

"This beautifully articulated book took this non-runner on a fast-paced journey up and down as I laughed and cried my way to the finish line. What an incredibly powerful experience, almost inspiring me to run. Definitely inspiring me to write!"

Jo Watson, Founder of adisorder4everyone.com,
Editor of Drop the Disorder and We are the Change-Makers.

"An antidote to impostor syndrome and a balm for those seeking connection in a fractured society, this is a fascinating and inspiring running story with universal appeal."

Lisa Jackson, author of
Running Made Easy and Your Pace or Mine?

"A brilliant read. Emotionally raw in places. Really, really good!"

Angela Gilmour, Gateshead Harrier,
Commonwealth Gold Medallist and Olympian.

MAKIN A MACKEM

Julie Carter

Published in 2023 by Mindfell

Copyright © 2023 Julie Carter

Julie Carter has asserted her right to be identified as the author of this Work in accordance with the Copyright, Designs and Patents Act 1988

ISBN Paperback: 978-1-9999554-5-8
Ebook: 978-1-9999554-6-5

This is a memoir, based on my lived experience. I have tried to recreate events and conversations from my memories of them, to the best of my ability. In order to maintain their anonymity, in a minority of instances I have changed the names of individuals.

A CIP catalogue copy of this book can be found in the British Library.

Published with the help of Indie Authors World
www.indieauthorsworld.com

IndieAuthors
World

Contents

Day Three

'…the fault, dear Brutus
Lies not in our stars but in ourselves that we are underlings.'

William Shakespeare, *Julius Caesar*

This book is dedicated to each and every Gateshead Harrier, past, present and future.

J. NOWELL
FOUNDER

"Think big deeds and you will grow"

From the Gateshead Harriers Handbook

A Short History of Two Tribes—
Mackems and Geordies

Mackems are people from Sunderland, once the greatest shipbuilding port in the world, and a place which supported the Scottish Jacobites, the 'Blue Macs', in their uprising against the English monarchy in 1745. The traditionally rebellious Mackems also supported the Parliamentarians in the English Civil War. Tynesiders are known as Geordies because they were on the other side and supported King George II against the rebels. Sunderland and Tyneside are only 10 miles apart but the rivalry between Geordies and Mackems originated long before their duels in football.

What happens when a Geordie marries a Mackem? One outcome of such a match was me.

Day One

Makin a Mackem

You need a long time to mak a Mackem—
It takes buckets and spades and Seaburn beach
      and holding to dreams
             that are miles out of reach.

It takes Roker Pier and 'Haway the Lads'
      and late-night beatings of mams by dads.
It takes pints of cider and vats of Blue Nun;
      knowing when to hide and when to run.

It takes courage and patience
      and the News O' The World,
          and a clout round the lugs
    when 'er tongue's unfurled.

But when she is welded—
      the Mackem is made;
she's as soft as a bairn
      and as hard as nails.

As hard as a nail
      that waits for the hammer,
          as soft as the dream
             that once began 'er.

1 *Not Drowning but Swimming*

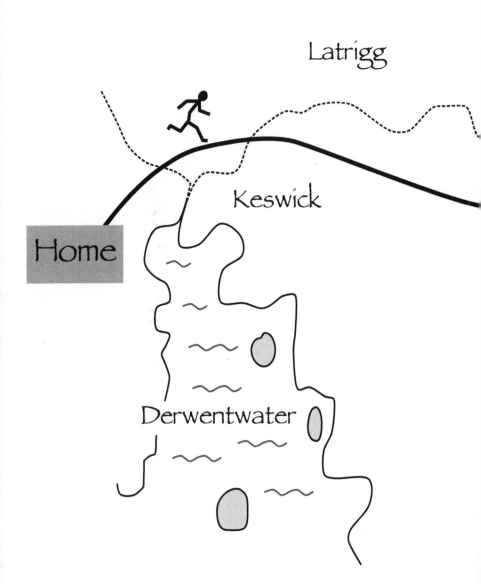

Latrigg

Keswick

Home

Derwentwater

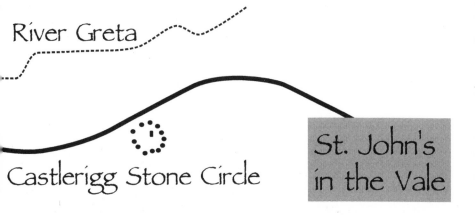

River Greta

Castlerigg Stone Circle

St. John's in the Vale

... there are tides in the body

Virginia Woolf, Mrs Dalloway

T he standing stones remain aloof in their circle as I run past in the pre-dawn gloom. It feels as if the whole world has been stood stock-still for a very long time. Time has gone weird since the lockdown in March. It is September 2020, and now it feels good for my body to be on the move; I can only ever make sense of anything when I'm on the move.

Sometimes I come up here just to be near the stones and to run my fingers over them, as if to read some braille-encoded story of how and why they came to be here. This morning I run on past them, following the small beam of light from my head torch. I am in my own world. The stone hulks congregate in their circle the same way they have for five thousand years. They just stand there, unmoved by the mountains that encircle them. A circle of stones within a circle of fells. The sounds of pattering trainers on the tarmac lane, and the pull and release of air in and out of my lungs, are almost drowned out by the insistent easterly wind, as the first pale hint of dawn creeps towards me. The Neolithic stone circle at Castlerigg is less than four miles from my house near Keswick in the Lake District. I've been running for only half an hour since leaving our front door. Being up here in early mornings or late evenings, without the usual daytime tourists, when these great hulking stones are left to themselves, I always feel they might confer. The stones remind me of Tolkien's tree-like 'Ents', those sentient inhabitants of Middle-Earth, which took on the forms of the beings it was their mission to save. In *The Lord of the Rings*, the

Ents protected the trees from felling. These stones—I imagine them holding counsel and enacting peculiar practices behind our backs in the darker hours, making plans to save the fabric of the planet from the evil destructive humans. If ever there was a time to catch them at it, surely it would be now, in this hinted grey half-dawn. But no. The stones are still and silent, and I run on past them.

This old and mysterious feeling I get at Castlerigg contains a nostalgia for lost kinds of knowledge and a yearning to reknit severed connections. The stones themselves may be indifferent, but they exert a gravitational pull on my being, a desire to know who the people were who built the circle. There is a longing within me, a need to be of a lineage, to belong to a place and tribe. The longer I live, the more I want this. These people who built the circle, I ponder about them. Were their lives a desperate struggle, plagued with disease and straitjacketed by superstition? Or were they knowledge seekers who held different values, who didn't believe in total human dominion? Did they see themselves as the top of a hierarchy of life, or as participants in an ecosystem enmeshed in natural cycles? Maybe they had different concepts of what is beautiful, and what is ugly; what is painful and what brings comfort. Whoever they were, if they have descendants alive today then the overwhelming likelihood is that I am one of them.

Genetic surveys have shown that we only have to trace back a thousand years to find that all Europeans have family relations in common. Every European alive a thousand years ago who has descendants alive today is an ancestor of all present-day humans of European lineage. And every person alive on the planet five thousand years ago, who has passed some of their DNA to presently living descendants, is an ancestor of everyone in the world. It's not that there was one couple, like an Adam and Eve, five thousand years ago. It's that the human family tree has woven itself together through entanglements and relationships. The human family tree doesn't just keep on branching, it keeps knitting itself together too. In fact, we are more of a tapestry than a tree. A five thousand year-old family tapestry which weaves in all eight billion of us. These people who built the stone circle—if any of the pattern of their DNA code survives today then a portion of it is inside my cells. The cells that make up the fabric of me and are the metabolic factories supplying the energy to keep me moving, to keep me running. If the circle builders have a living family, then I am in it.

It wasn't in my plan to linger to watch the dawn at the stones; I'll have to keep running. And the morning is going exactly as planned so far. The planning of this adventure hasn't only been about logistics. What will be felt on this run, what will be thought, and understood—in my controlling way I have tried to plan for all that too. In some way I intend this run to be an exorcism, a catharsis, a cleansing of my tarnished past. It isn't a penance; it is a pilgrimage.

And when I woke in the dark at 5.30 this morning everything was ready—my clothes and socks and trainers all laid out. The vest I had been sent in the post, designed over a hundred years ago by my ancestor, is white and red, with 'Gateshead Harriers' in black letters across the chest. I have black shorts and red socks chosen to match. No one in my athletic club will mind that for three days I will be in the colours of a different team. It troubles me that I will not be able to run the ninety-odd miles from my house in Cumbria to the stadium in Gateshead in one go. I have done much harder runs in the past, but my body is increasingly debilitated by a back problem which developed in my childhood, the outcome of some genetic wonkiness. And there is also the aftermath of a climbing accident in 2018, in which my pelvis was broken in several places, from my tailbone to my hip. Now anything longer than an hour or so of sustained running can easily become painfully gruelling.

I'm not greatly skilled in the art of compromise, but I'm hoping that if I split the journey into three days, with rests along the way, and I'm met by my partner with overnight stays in our van, then I might make it. It has felt difficult to explain to anybody what I am about to do and why. Because beneath the logistics of *the plan*, and my telling myself a story about why I'm doing this, I'm really not sure myself about the *why*. I just know that it must be done. The whole sense of why this journey is important to me is slightly mysterious. The idea of it was a feeling, which came from my innards.

Before leaving home this morning, while finishing my wake-up tea, always the best brew of the day, I pick up a scribbled list from the kitchen bench—things not to forget from the fridge and most importantly a special birthday cake out of the freezer which I made two days ago. I open the back door to stick my hand out and test the temperature, deciding if I need a jumper. It's always part of the ritual in the final few minutes before an important run or race. How many layers? Hat on or off? Gloves on hands or in pockets? It's a way of letting the mind occupy itself instead of worrying about what is ahead. Yet in these moments I don't feel I'm just doing normal stuff; I feel instead like I am acting someone else's part. I'm acting the part of someone who believes in themselves and believes, despite all the evidence to the contrary, that I can run a very long way. It's a strange feeling, but it's one I have learned to go along with. I know I'm acting but there have been glorious occasions when the acting has paid off. Faking it till I made it. But it feels like being two different people in the same moment.

Two minutes later I open the front door and adjust my head torch beam. Then forget my sleeping neighbours and laugh out loud. My friend Lesley, with whom I have shared many wild runs, is unexpectedly lurking outside in the dark.

'Couldn't let you go without a good send-off, Jules!'

We don't hug as the Covid virus is also lurking and that kind of thing is off-limits. But I do feel the love. The love that I have so often felt from the people I share my running with.

Our next-door neighbour, Nicky, is awake and waving from her upstairs window.

'Have a good 'n; good luck.'

Already I am lucky because there is a lull in the pandemic which has allowed me to set off. A kiss for my wife, Mandy, a pat for Moss the dog, and I run quietly into the dark. I turn the corner from our house and pass Derwent Hill, the outdoor centre where I came with my Sunderland school group at age 13; a week that changed my life. Then I run over the *wobbly bridge*—the little suspension foot-bridge over the River Derwent—which we used to jump up and down on when we were kids at Derwent Hill because we enjoyed the wobble. This morning I am alone in the pool of light from my head torch, with only the sound of my breathing and the inner voice of my thoughts for company. Why does a broken middle-aged woman have to run from Keswick to Gateshead? Maybe I'll figure things out, by the time I get there.

Running through the park in Keswick, in the pitch dark, I am in a strange in-between state, as if suspended between two worlds. I am running over intimate ground, but it feels new. I have run around this park hundreds of times during interval training sessions with my club mates. We would do six times one lap, which is a few metres over a kilometre, with two minutes' rest between each one, then go again—hard. We would regroup after each effort with bursting lungs and burning legs, then end by jogging home, happily chatting. This is my place. My habitat. Except this morning it feels like I have never been here before.

In everyday life I have come to appreciate this park as a symbol of democracy and human rights, right here under my feet. The enclosure acts, which started in the 1700s, led to terrific poverty in the whole of Britain. By the mid-nineteenth century, the people of Keswick had no access to outdoor public space. The trespass laws meant they were not free to roam, their living conditions were cramped, and cholera was common.

Fitz Park was created in an effort to improve matters and is held in trust, as it has been for over 130 years. This park is not just a park, it is community medicine. I run out of the park through the iron gates and along the old railway line, which was a profitable and busy link between Penrith and the West Coast until it was closed in the 1960s. For years it's been a gravel cycling track edged by mature trees but now, despite protests, it's being tarmacked, and the trees cut down. I run on. Up Chestnut Hill, which ups my heart rate, until I reach the circle of stones.

I was six years old, possibly seven, and I was triumphant. We almost had the beach to ourselves, under the big blue sky, our bodies soaking up the heat. Amble in Northumberland didn't often feel this luxurious. My mam held my hand as I emerged from the sea with a feeling of pure self-pride. With salt on my lips and the breeze in my hair, I let go and ran off to dance with the water's edge. My feet landed firm on the shining sand which was sprinkled with seashells sparkling like jewels. A distant dog barked congratulations and gulls squawked in celebration overhead. Once or twice, there was a whoosh and surge of a bigger wave rushing up the shore and the frothing water almost took my legs from under me. I felt fabulous and free, running along the waterline.

Mam was walking up to above the tideline to tell Dad, disinterestedly snoozing on his faded stripy deckchair, 'She can swim'. I could swim. No rubber ring, no arm bands. I could swim and the world was glorious. Life wouldn't be the same now that I could swim—now that miracles could happen. My mam, in her bright orange bathing costume, had been close and attentive and I felt a special kind of touch under my tummy. Mam's hands had all the gentleness of someone who was setting a butterfly to flight. She calmed and reassured me, going through practising the arms and then the legs, and I giggled at the legs, thinking it hilarious to kick like a frog.

And slowly, but at just the right moment, she let go but kept there, very close, and telling me I was alright. I *was* alright, swimming head-up breaststroke in the English North Sea on a sunny summer morning. What was even more amazing, after my triumph, and having been guided back to a standing depth by Mam, was that after a minute I tried it again—and I could still do it! The feeling of that first visceral eureka would never leave my body.

'I can do it, I can do it, I can do it!'

Mam didn't get much response from the deckchair but when she came back down to the water, we went back in again. I couldn't get enough of the feeling, hopping through the waves, arms reaching high above my head to stave off the cold as the sea crept up my little sun-baked body. When the water hit my chest with an uncontrollable gasp I had to surrender. What a feeling—to be taken, to allow the water to take me off my feet. A deep breath, head up, and trust. Trust the water. Trust my mam. Trust myself. Weightless and enveloped, arms and legs moving through the shifting sea as the sun's rays burned into the back of my neck.

Swimming in reach of the shore but looking seaward, being in the body of water that stretched all the way to Coquet Island with its lighthouse. Only a mile away, the island looked to be on the edge of the world. I used to like it on foggy nights, snuggled under heavy woolly blankets in the caravan, when the lighthouse foghorn sounded. It was eerie and comforting at the same time; signalling danger but there to be a guide to safe passage as each boom died away to an echo across the water, never quite ending. My body was under the blankets and my imagination was out there, in a spooky serenity of fog on the sea, in the night.

But now on this abnormally hot day I was in the same sea, the same sailor-travelled sea, the very same sea where my mam had swum when she was a child. As I moved through and with the water, I could feel the mysterious motion of the waves and the outgoing tide and I was cradled, held in the rocking of the sea. 'Relax,' whispered the water, 'I've got you'.

For a moment I almost forgot my mam was still nearby watching.

'Eeeee, yu dee-in smashing pet! There yu go. That's marvellous. Yu swimmin smashing! Come on. Wull gan out now. Yu divunt want te get cold.'

'Can wu come tomorra, Mam?'

'Wi eye pet, course wu can. Eee I'm proud of yu! Yuv done well pet.'

Did life get any better—was it possible to get higher than on the pleasure of approval?

'Can wu pick some willicks after dinner, Mam? The tide ull be properly oot b' then.'

'Yes pet. Run up there and wake yu dad up. He's bloody hopeless.'

My legs felt heavy as they sank into the pale soft sand at the top of the beach. Dad was still asleep with his mouth hanging open and his beer gut overhanging his cream-coloured trousers. Without a shirt, his hairy torso had turned bright red and looked like a roasting pig. I rattled the deckchair's wooden slats—very gently, in case it collapsed.

'Dad, I'm hungry and yuv been asleep for ages. Can wu gan for wu dinners?'

We gathered our stuff together for the short walk through the sand dunes back to the caravan. We were an incongruous alliance, wrestling ramshackle beach luggage.

Mam couldn't stand his incompetence. 'Yu bloody hopeless, Vernon. Yu cannot even fold up a deckchair. An divunt moan to me yuv got sunburnt. Yu lump a' useless fat.'

'I'll show yu who's bloody hopeless, woman.'

And he would. As later in the dark my usually stubborn mam became helpless, and would scream and cry, and swear and struggle, then plead in vain.

'Gerroff yu bastard, I cannot stand yu, yu'll kill uz, no, no, ye bastard gerroff.'

While he would force himself inside her, telling her to shut up, or he'd shut her up for good, while three feet away on the other side of a flimsy plywood partition, I would rock in my caravan bunk to the rhythm of his rape, lie awake to his snores, and get up in the morning, frozen in shame, feeling that if only I could try harder, be better, somehow this would not happen. But I always failed—because it always did.

Some mornings, while he was out getting a paper, Mam would gather herself together and try to reassure me. 'I'm sorry pet. Don't worry though—not all men are like yu dad. Du yu want Cornflakes or Rice Crispies?'

Then Dad would come back from the shop with sweets or a new kite or some crayons and paper. One time he brought me a painted wooden bird on a stick which made a funny pecking motion when a string was pulled. These were extravagances which Mam disapproved of. As a lump of white lard melted to translucent grease in the pan on the Calor Gas stove she would plonk in his bread to fry. And nothing else was said.

By the time I'm at the top of the hill, just beyond the stone circle, a thin strip of light frills the horizon far out to the east beyond the fells. Familiar places can feel strange at times when something special or shocking is happening—a wedding day, a funeral, a pandemic evolving, the threat of war. Habitat is not a stage-set for our life-scenes but a participant in the acting out.

I am disturbed by this peculiar feeling of the unfamiliar familiar through which I am running. Soon I might wake from the dream to the morning tea and realise I am yet to start running. I am able to accept that getting ready is performed in a different mind-space; but once I start running, the ephemeral usually disappears with each grounding connection of foot on earth. Living through the lockdown and restrictions of the previous months, the fears and insecurities, maybe the oddness of the times is playing into the weirdness of my feelings.

The first thing a brain automatically does when it encounters something is to ask 'Have I seen this before? Do I know what this is? What is it like?' Our brains are doing this pattern-matching all the time. When I see my running shoes sitting outside our back door, I don't have to think about what they are and what they mean. We work on a system of learned pattern recognition. But today a sort of amnesia has taken hold of me. It is a curious and altering feeling, a sense that the world is bewilderingly odd, and that the oddness truly is reality. I remember that the physicist and Nobel Laureate, Richard Feynman, openly admitted to not understanding his own work and said: 'If you think you understand quantum mechanics, you don't understand quantum mechanics.' He cautioned against always trying to understand the world in terms of something familiar. Oddness is not a problem; it's the way things truly are, and I find that paradoxically calming. It's alright, it's not me—the world is strange—it's genuinely strange—it's okay to feel this. The touch of foot on tarmac, left and right, left and right, left and right, is a kind of reassurance.

Seeking confirmation of something trustworthy, I look over my shoulder to glimpse the emerging shape of the little hill of Latrigg. Latrigg is only a little over a thousand feet high but its presence in the lives of most of us Keswick runners is huge. This hill has been the host of so many hard-won training efforts by generations of athletes over decades. During the Covid lockdown, Latrigg became known as the 'Keswick Runners' Social Club'. If we feel lonely, we just go for a run up Latrigg from our own front doors and there will be a friend on the path to smile at and chat to. Even at night. In fact it's easier then because our head torches give us away.

Latrigg is a hill with every gradient and surface a runner could want, for uphill strength and speed training, for downhill technique, for nice easy jaunts through the woods above the river, for a summit view of the whole of Derwentwater and Borrowdale and beyond. I have strolled up there via the short route at the back, in times of convalescence, for myself and for friends seeking comfort when ill or injured, and even with my mother in her final years of heart failure. I've run in thrilling intense races up Latrigg. I've read a poem by the bench near the top for my friends Jenn and Carl who got married up there. We all assembled on a glorious summer day for the bride and groom who had run up from home in a great posse of yellow Keswick vests, Carl clutching a carrier bag with a dress for Jenn and a shirt and tie for himself which they quickly slipped on over the top of their running kit. And they looked gorgeous. During the ceremony it was as if Latrigg held up Jenn and Carl and all their friends as you would hold up a crystal to sparkle in the sunlight.

The shape of Latrigg emerging from the dark is soon left behind as I speed down the hill to St John's in the Vale and towards my breakfast. Around the next bend in the narrow road, I can see a few scattered lights in the farms and houses below me in the valley. That's where I'm hoping that Mandy will be waiting. I used to be fabulous at running downhill but now downhill on tarmac is pretty sore on my pelvis. No—I tell myself not to think about that. I'm here now, this morning, and that's all that matters. The steep sides of Clough Head and Great Dodd, with their deep mysterious gullies, are appearing from the dark. Along those summits are well-worn grassy paths which are easy to run on, but on their slopes below there is a rarely visited world of tangled nooks and ravines. I enjoy peering at them, but I'll not be going up there today. The lights are close now and I'm hoping that within the next ten minutes I'll be enjoying another mug of tea.

Accidents

To begin—energy, matter and time expanded into nothing—which did
not exist.

A uniform universe acquired a history by mutating parameters, evolving
a cosmos.
A wobble in the maths made gravity greedy for stuff, which coalesced
                                        like lumps in custard.

Stars, planets, suns, moons, air, oceans, raindrops, earth and trees, love
and me.
Born and dying, in my time passing, the future already knows my end—
                                        my agency is in doubt.

I am a completely random, absolutely unique, perfect imperfection.
I cried when my mother told me I was a mistake. Now I understand the
universal joke
                                        I laugh with all my heart.

2 *Don't Run—*
It's Dangerous

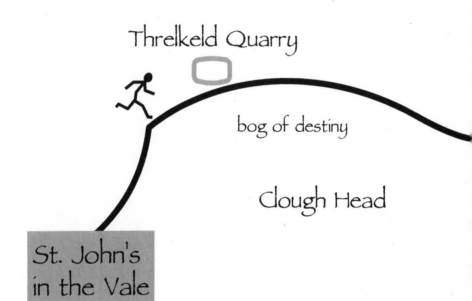

Threlkeld Quarry

bog of destiny

Clough Head

St. John's
in the Vale

old Coach Road

Dockray

Everything can be taken from a man but… the last of the human freedoms— to choose one's attitude in any given set of circumstances, to choose one's own way.

Victor Frankl, Man's Search for Meaning

I switch off my torch, now that the daylight has properly arrived, and I find Mandy parked up outside our friends' cottage in St John's in the Vale. The kettle is boiled on the van stove, the porridge is made, but I'll only eat half a bowl as I'll have to set off running again straight away and don't want to make myself feel sick. I get very edgy when I think I might not have food available and I used to think it was healthy for a runner to be so concerned with their fuel supply. Although I'm not as skinny as a lot of runners, you couldn't call me overweight at five-foot-three and eight and a half stone. I assumed my approach to food was fine. I need energy to run—of course I need to eat a lot. But the older I get, the more my guts play up.

My friend Lesley, who saw me off earlier, is a brilliant fellrunner and her approach is to hardly eat anything on long runs. I used to think she was a bit crazy but now I think she's on to something. All this eating while running doesn't make sense. The hormones and blood distribution we need while digesting are completely different to those needed for action. We have not evolved to run and digest at the same time. If I didn't eat anything during the days between now and Gateshead and only drank water I would still make it, because at least 20 per cent of my bodyweight is energy stored as fat. If I desisted from eating while running then I could train my metabolism to burn fat and use its reserves more effectively and then replenish afterwards when it's time to *rest and digest*. It might be a better idea to just eat in the evenings when I've stopped running. But I was really looking forward to this porridge and it tastes lovely.

There were longer and less tarmacked routes I could have taken from my house to my breakfast but I was glad to have run near the Castlerigg stones. The expansion of time they create in my mind makes me feel more like a thread in a living tapestry than a disconnected person bent on individual goals. Long-distance running is the ultimate symbol of single-minded endeavour. Running allows me to retreat. But the retreat is from the overstimulated buzz of my life and it is an attempt to weave myself back into the world, to forge a reliable sense of connection. I am beginning to see my journeys as a kind of land art. Creations which are melds of fells and paths and a living body. On this run my quest is to understand more about what I have inherited, and also about what I might pass on.

As a writer my legacy depends on reaching people with words. I worry about the destructive language which seems to pervade running culture. Phrases like 'Smash it!', 'Destroy it!', 'You're an animal!', 'Beast', are all over our club social media these days. When words such as 'pulverise' and 'annihilate' are used about rivals and about the fells themselves, our sport begins to sound like a boxing match or a violent online game. Fellrunners are hungry for a challenge; and because the pandemic has caused a lot of race cancellations many have turned their attention to breaking individual time records for long-distance routes. Even as a seasoned long-distancer myself, I am in awe of many of their runs and full of admiration for their endurance. But I question what the language is saying about these endeavours. Are these wonderful journeys of body and soul really about breaking and smashing things? And the now popular acronym for 'Fastest Known Time' (FKT) causes an unfortunate pattern match in the language centres of most English speakers' brains. Are we fucking something here or are we creating something? Instead of saying 'go smash it', maybe we could say 'go love it!' or 'go out there and be gorgeous.'

For now, I'm just enjoying the porridge and the chat with two friends who live nearby as they huddle bleary-eyed beside the van in their down jackets. They're not usually up this early but I have only seen them briefly in the street since the beginning of the pandemic, so it's good to catch up.

'Eee, yu shouldn't run like that pet! It's dangerous! Get that sand swept up. Worra mess.'

I had burst in through the caravan door, breathless, bringing in remnants of the beach that were clinging to my shoes. I'd run over the dunes as fast as I could—just for the feel of it. In my memory I am about eight or nine and I'd begun to notice things when I ran. I'd started to notice that feeling of freedom; the sensation of controlling my energy and my breath and being just on the edge of something. On the edge of not being able to keep going, but keeping going anyway; being patient for every inhalation of oxygen, legs and heart and lungs finding an only-just-manageable speed. I'd begun to notice how it felt for all the knots in my guts to loosen, and to feel warmed through by the rhythm of my own heartbeat. The fear of the world that held me frozen would melt away whenever I ran. But that good feeling did not last long as I stood in the caravan, defenceless against my mother's telling-off. Breathless and bewildered, I wanted to communicate to her that it was possible, if only for a few minutes, or seconds, even for someone as small and shy as me, to feel free. Obedient and mute, I got the brush and dustpan from the cupboard, as perhaps the most essential penny of my life just dropped. The knowing that I can create my own moments of freedom—no matter what.

The older I got, the more the disconnect between Mam and me grew. She told me I had been 'a mistake' but I was far too naïve to understand what she meant by it. All I knew was that life was very spiky and edgy, that something felt fundamentally wrong, and that I was deeply implicated in the wrongness. The beautiful feeling of wet sand grains under my feet, the physical connection with the beach, these were comfort. I always loved running on the beach in any weather. Mam never bothered about me going out in the rain, saying that 'it doesn't go beyond the skin'. Which puzzled me because, as far as I was concerned, everything went beyond the skin. My skin soaked up the prickly sensation of my mother's fear and heartbreak. The feeling of sand and seawater on my body was balm. I always held onto the hope of more of those important miracles, those sun-filled summery moments—like when she taught me to swim. The lack of them made me pull into myself, and feel cold inside, like the sea on a grey winter day.

On the beach, picking willicks to eat for tea, and watching all the creatures in the rock pools, and the way different birds had particular habits along the shore—all that gave me a fascination with the weirdness of other living beings. Something as fleshy and exotic as a starfish, with its thousands of juicy little suckers, and something as delicately graceful and fleeting as a common tern winging over the waves, dart-shaped and defiant—that these beings should inhabit my world was astonishing. I wanted to learn about them, to know their names, the details of how they went about life. And I was convinced it would all be in books. Mam wasn't keen on that kind of learning. There was an unstated message that I should fit into what was expected, not try too hard to get above myself—it would only lead to disappointment. But there was an alluring strangeness in those creatures that kept my curiosity going, and later at school I read in an encyclopaedia that some birds fly for thousands of miles every year and always know where they are. Such confidence, such self-belief.

In primary school, at lunchtimes, when other kids would hop-scotch together, or do weird things like stone-paper-scissors, which I didn't understand, I would spend my time running up and down the playground, along the edge of the rough concrete, needing the effort of it to tolerate the tension inside me. Before the days when kids who were a bit different had to be given labels, I was allowed to be me without comment. In the playground, I ran to drink the fresh air, feel it go down the back of my throat, like quenching a thirst. But my running was never much use when it came to games lessons. Our teacher hated me because I sat in her class and got full marks on every written test she meted out, and finished in half the time of my classmates, while making a point of never saying anything at all to her. Mrs Fawcett could not get a word out of me.

Her idea of a PE lesson would be for the boys to play football or cricket and the girls to watch. But then, in the last term of primary, there was a push for the whole class to get our British Association of Gymnastics certificates. Getting ready was mayhem as we would all get changed at our classroom desks, boys and girls together, and someone was always short of something and had to ratch through a smelly box of ragged spares. But we'd reached the stage when feminine bodies were becoming something of an issue. Entering puberty, we were no longer simply ourselves as we turned into objects of public interest. In deference to decency, the girls who were developing curves would go into the store cupboard to change, including my friend Ann, and one day I followed her in but was quickly turned around by Mrs Fawcett.

'Get back out of there, Julie Carter. You. If only you could be like Ann. You're nothing like her, you'll never be like her. Get back out. You child—I wonder if you'll ever grow up.'

Our disrespect was completely mutual.

As we marched to the hall, I felt sick from the smell of wood and leather—the gym horse, the polished floor, the pain, the embarrassment. Mrs Fawcett said we had to get ten exercises ticked off. One of them was called 'crab', where you faced the ceiling, torso in the air and back arched, with feet and hands on the ground. For weeks I tried to get the better of the crab and my friends would stand next to me and try to help me.

'Go on Julie, it's easy, get yer hands down flat and just push yer belly up.'

And I would push and collapse, ungracefully defeated, in a heap, again. I managed the other exercises, even the vaulting of that sinister hard horse, but the crab was never conquered. In the end everyone except me was given a cloth badge and Mrs Fawcett supervised the class as they were proudly sewn onto PE shirts while I was tasked with sorting out her store cupboard. I didn't understand why my back hurt so much, why it was impossible for me to achieve a *crab*, and why no amount of effort on my part could alter the situation. I was in my twenties before a doctor diagnosed the growth problem in my spine, called Scheuermann's disease. Something had gone a bit wrong in my genes. My spine was already curved forward in primary school and was destined to grow more so.

'Sit up straight Julie, I won't tell you again.'

That was the mantra recited throughout my childhood, over and over. But I've never been able to sit up straight, it's just not how I'm built. I tried hard—and failed constantly.

Leaving the breakfast stop, the next part of my journey will be along the Old Coach Road which runs under Clough Head, a much more beautiful fell than its name suggests. I've crossed this track hundreds of times but have never run along it, since it doesn't link the hills that a fellrunner usually inhabits. It looked straightforward on the map though, and I'm reassured by my breakfast-time friend, who just happens to be a Geordie, clutching his hot coffee mug and smiling.

'Why yes, it's a big track all the way to Dockray. It's pretty bleak up there, mind Jules. Rather you than me. Did you know Dockray is where Fred Hoyle used to live?'

It doesn't surprise me that my friend knows all about the controversial twentieth-century astromer Fred Hoyle, a man who discovered much about how stars are made. My Geordie marra has a lump of meteorite on a table in his living room. Something not from this planet, just sitting there on his table. While finishing off the porridge, deciding I can manage the other half bowl after all, I am treated to a summary of how Hoyle didn't believe the universe had a start and end in time. It's definitely expanding but there are explanations for the expansion of the universe, other than the 'Big Bang Theory', according to Fred Hoyle, who thought this idea was a kind of rehash of Genesis and that the biblical creation story had tainted the collective scientific imagination.

Which is all very fascinating but I do need to set off across the bleak moor soon and I hope it hasn't expanded too much in the time it has taken me to have breakfast. I reassure myself that any such expansion will go unnoticed, since if the moor has got bigger than so will I and all the measurable objects around us, so it will still be about six miles to Dockray. I set off and, closing the gate, look back to see our dog Moss gazing longingly, wondering why she isn't invited. I'm tempted to open the gate again and call her through but I'm not sure this track will be good for her old paws. Moss the hound is at the stage in life where her motivation and love of running are as keen as ever; but when she has done too much, the next day she struggles out of her bed and is obviously in pain. When I'm doing something that I think won't be good for her and she sees me leave, she fixes me with a quiet intent stare.

'I'm sorry Moss. Go back. Mandy will take you for a little walk.'

She never whines or barks—just stands still with a longing look, and watches me go.

As I follow the Old Coach Road eastwards, I'm expecting it to be easy but find the running is harder underfoot than on the open fell. Rutted water-worn gutters and awkward rocky ballast alternate with gluey mud which attaches itself in great heavy clods to my trainers. I have to kick it off, otherwise I feel like I'm running in platform heels. I'm faced with a poor choice of running surface: awkward loose rubble, thick glue-mud or the boggy reedy ground to the side of the track. Still I'm glad I'm not on top of a fell somewhere—it would be hard to stand up on any summit in this wind. Grey clouds are whisking overhead but show no sign of dispensing rain.

The track climbs steadily uphill until it forks near a small quarry. Being naturally lazy, and optimistic, I think the lower track must be the right one, and press on, but within a mile I realise where I am. I'm far too low on the fellside, with the Coach Road way above me. I have come out on the little trod which is part of the Bob Graham Round route as it climbs out of Threlkeld towards Clough Head. I know this reedy bog too well. There is no unfamiliarity now and I can't believe I have ended up here, again. This is the same reedy bog I trudged through so many times on practice runs for my 'Bob Graham Round'—a fellrunning loop of the Lake District which involves visiting forty-two summits in under twenty-four hours. When fairly new to fellrunning at the age of forty-one, I was out training with two friends, ploughing through this same reedy bog one drizzly morning, listening to their conversation, too exhausted by my 'Ministry of Funny Walks' technique to say much myself, when at this very spot, something important happened.

Sam happened to ask Dave if he was going to do a 'fifty at fifty'. I couldn't help but ask what that was—*fifty at fifty*?

'It's all the forty-two Bob Graham Round summits plus an extra eight, when you are over fifty years old.'

The moment these words passed Sam's vocal cords and flew out into the damp fellside air, I knew that was something I wanted to do. I was thinking 'I'll do the BG when I'm forty-two and then I'll do fifty when I'm fifty'. What puzzles me is where these notions come from with such certitude. It's as if I have no choice in the matter. Something in my body, right in the centre of me, makes a choice—'Yes. Yes. I'll do that, for sure.' Whatever I think, by which I mean whatever strings of internal words my brain can assemble, seems peripheral. It's somewhere in the guts of me where the real decisions happen. And now, enmeshed in the same frustrating damn reeds again, I am annoyed that I've lost all the extra time and effort, because if I'd just gone on the top track I wouldn't be back in the bog. But at least the *funny walks* trudge back up the hill is familiar. And I am laughing, as I re-christen the place: *The Bog of Destiny.*

In secondary school we had a real **PE** teacher and her name was Mrs B. Ware. As a squinty-eyed, misshapen kid with a bad back, no 3-D vision, no coordination and no idea, games lessons were just a kind of torture I had to endure—with one outstanding exception. Once a term, we had to do the cross-country run. As we lined up on the school playing field, the class had all the enthusiasm of a bunch of prisoners being put to work. Once around the corner, the subversion would begin. Plots hatched about how long to hide for and where. Who had fags and where it would be safest to go for a smoke. Would there be time to nip into the newsagent at the bottom of Durham Road bank for a quick light-fingered gleaning of Mars Bars? There was only one person stupid enough to run the course properly, and of course I would always win. I never had an answer when my friends asked me 'why?'. My body and soul loved running; it was a mystery to me too. I asked Mrs Ware about cross-country.

'Is it a real sport Miss?'

This was the one time I mustered the courage to speak to my terrifying teacher. She told me there was a town cross-country race the following week after school and, if I could get myself there, she could arrange for my name to be put on the list. This was a revelation. I could go to a race and there might be other freaks like me who enjoyed running too. I didn't know how to get to the other school across town but somehow figured out the bus numbers and arrived in my Aertex top, gym skirt and pumps. I had never seen a real race of any sort. I gave my name to the teacher in charge who made a note on her clipboard.

'You'd better hurry up and get changed pet, your age group will be called in ten minutes.'

I didn't know what to say. I *was* changed. Everyone else had real running kit on, proper shorts and vests and cross-country shoes with spikes in the soles. Humiliated before we had even started, I could only just hold back my tears as we ran off, my pumps slithering pathetically in the mud. On the first incline I was on the ground. Struggling to my feet in a miserable mix of shame and disappointment, I finished the race, not last but almost. I wasn't even sure I could remember which bus to get back home but would rather have died than ask anyone. Nobody else was getting the bus, they all had parents holding tracksuit tops and taking them home in cars. When I did get home, I never told my mam and dad where I'd been. I didn't want to get told off and I realised I had been stupid. I had ventured into a world where I didn't belong. Thankfully when we next had PE, Mrs B. Ware said nothing about it either. I had learnt my lesson. Running was out of my league. Maybe Mam was right. Running was dangerous.

Back on the rubbly Coach Road I wonder what it would be like travelling in a horse-drawn coach instead of in a pair of trainers. The road would have been a thoroughfare at one time. It's higher up the valley side than the main A66 but it avoids some major river crossings which are now spanned by big concrete bridges carrying the modern road. The Coach Road is on maps from the early 1700s, but it must have been a travel route long before that. I'm progressing faster and starting to enjoy the running, as my feet tune in to how to negotiate the awkward track. Below me is Threlkeld Quarry, which is now a mining museum with a little steam railway. Just above it, in certain lights, you can see the outlines of ancient enclosures with remnants of cairns and huts dating from the Bronze Age. Ancient bone and charcoal were excavated from the site in 1901, but now it's left, not to be further disturbed.

Ancestors are never far away. I wonder how far those generations, long before written records, used to travel. The reedy bog would have been woodland then. Did these ancestors run? How did they run; when did they run; how far did they run and why? Was it all for hunting or was some of it travelling for other reasons, or escaping, and if escaping what were they running from? They must have run. It's not a modern invention. And what did they know about the Big Bang and the flow of time? They had theories and creation stories, just like we do. Thinking about those ancient people as I push on against the strong easterly wind, I begin to feel warmer, a kind of relaxation in my body. I do feel a bit lonely up here but thinking about these ancestors reminds me that long journeys on foot aren't remarkable at all. It's the normality of twenty-first century life, A-roads and cars, the internet and my synthetic running shoes, which are truly unusual.

Memories flicker like a celluloid movie played too slowly, so that each frame becomes a still. It was the summer that my dad's mother came up with her new husband to our caravan in Amble for the six-week school holidays. I had no siblings to amuse me by then; my two elder brothers had flown the nest in their late teens while I was still at primary school. My brothers were like mystical beings to me then; stronger and more resourceful than I could ever dream of being. They'd sometimes arrive on their motorbikes with girlfriends and stay the occasional night. I was in awe of their strength and independence and I wanted to be like them. But I was too young, and I was a girl.

Dad was at work in the week and came to the caravan every Friday for the weekend. Running down to the village to meet his bus, wondering if he had brought me a tube of fruit pastels or a bar of fruit and nut chocolate, I knew I would be safe while he was there, until he left again on Monday morning. When he wasn't drunk he was usually very quiet, withdrawn but kind to me, and that suited me fine. On weekdays, when he wasn't there, Mam and my grandmother were conspiratorial, often wanting to go shopping or out on the bus somewhere. They said I was better off staying with Grandma's new husband who would just be sleeping or reading the paper, and I could do what I wanted.

It happened many times, I can't say how many. Sometimes there was blood, which I washed out or made an excuse about if remnants were discovered. He would make me lie down on the bottom bunk, which Mam had left the plastic cover on because she often put our luggage on there when packing and wanted to keep the mattress clean. The old man would take off his big dirty-white underpants with shitty skid marks.

'You can't tell anyone. This is our secret. If you tell anyone, very bad things will happen to you. You understand that, don't you? I know you're a good girl'.

I tried to push him off, to escape out the door, but he would have me trapped. I remember the thin wooden beading down the seams of the caravan walls, with little heads of tiny nails, spaced evenly every few inches, from which a small streak of black diffused into the wood. I remember the door to the bunk room, the tarnished ribbed handle that was still partly covered with flecks of gold-coloured paint. The door sneck was a little white ball which made a click into its socket. Door snecks and tacks in plywood—indelible photographs. The other memories, the shock of his dick, the tearing pain, the sticky spunk; those memories seem less vivd than the click of a door sneck, or tacks in plywood.

My mam was only eleven years old when her own mam died. It always surprised me how keen she was to spend time with her mother-in-law who seemed a reckless kind of woman. But maybe, in missing out on being mothered, my mam was still seeking to fill a mother-shaped emptiness. That summer the two of them seemed to have something which Mam wanted very much, and from which I felt very excluded. I overheard them talking about sex. My grandmother had been through a few husbands and I never quite understood who my dad's dad was. She was telling my mam how, even though she was in her seventies, she still enjoyed sex, and how the new husband might be old and portly but 'He's still a real man with a man's needs. That's why I married him. I wanted a bloke who can still perform.'

I was eleven myself that summer. Life went on. I became very quiet indeed. Everyone thought I was just a very shy kid who didn't have anything to say.

If you were so minded you could call the moor to the north-east of Clough Head bleak. It's a landscape stripped bare by centuries of grazing. I haven't seen or heard a bird or any other animal, but it's still very windy so maybe they are all taking shelter. Even the Herdwick sheep, our woolly accomplices in deforestation, are nowhere to be seen.

Approaching a gate across the track, I can see two people in the distance coming towards me. It's funny how I often feel shy, meeting strangers like this. I'm apprehensive that they might think I ought not to be out here running on my own. Like I'm doing something transgressive. It reminds me of an account of an early female mountaineer in the nineteenth century, hiding behind rocks during a walk to the summit of Snowdon to avoid the chastisement of the *official* guides. There is a feeling that I don't quite have the right somehow, to just run alone in quiet places. Like the deer in the woods—I always want to run away when someone appears. Running on the fells near my own house, my very familiar fells, I don't get this feeling so much. Knowing each turn of trod, there is a familiarity and strength of bond between my body and my habitat, where I run in all weathers, month in and year out. When I'm on new territory there's no lack of confidence about navigating or moving over difficult ground in hard conditions. I know how to do this stuff. But there is a fear, which I think is about being judged, as being out of place. Like I don't have a right to this kind of freedom. But then I think about my beloved Latrigg again because it was on this hill that one of the first acts of the right-to-roam movement took place in England, forty-five years before the more famous Kinder Trespass in Derbyshire.

On Saturday 1st October 1887 the Keswick stationmaster Henry Irwin Jenkinson stood at the foot of Latrigg and addressed a gathering of 2,500 people, including 'a good muster of ladies'. The crowd then peacefully walked to the summit, asserting their right to walk on paths which had been barricaded off by the landowner.

And the asserters dismantled the barriers peacefully and carefully and even the children were not allowed to pick a berry to show their respect to the property owner, Mr Spedding. And in his letter in the *Manchester Guardian* on 3rd October, Jenkinson testified:

> '*Not an ill word was spoken, not a blade of grass was broken [...]*
> *Never did a crowd of people meet more as a family, and more*
> *exemplify that there is a groundwork of goodness at the bottom of*
> *all human nature.*'

Henry Irwin Jenkinson wasn't just a local hero but a man who co-founded a movement which asserted access to the countryside and changed the lives of millions. When I'm on runs up Latrigg and arrive, sweaty and breathless, at the summit, I take a moment to look across to Borrowdale and thank Henry Irwin Jenkinson for what he passed on to us. I take strength from reflecting on Jenkinson standing in front of the crowd and making them pledge good behaviour, turning the dispossessed into *asserters*. I love to imagine the asserters, all 2,500 of them. I think of them on the terrace path, imagine I can hear their voices and feel their excitement. I have so much freedom—because of them.

With blurry vision from the eye-watering wind, I had not realised at first that the people approaching are no strangers. Carl and Jenn are walking slowly, as Jenn's baby is expected to enter the world any day now. Being almost nine months pregnant hasn't stopped my friend getting out of bed for a wild walk on a windy morning, in the back end of beyond, to encourage me on my way. We are the only ones up here on the moor. Me and two champion fellrunners and their unborn child. The morning belongs to the four of us, and I start to feel an inner *yes* about what I am doing on this run. Yes—it's right, it makes sense, of course it does. My friends seem to get it, even if I'm not sure. I have lived my life trying to ignore, deny and escape from all that I believe I have inherited. This run is an attempt to re-examine all that. Because even though I get on with the business of living to the best of my abilities, I carry a sense that I come from badness and was grown in badness. It is a childlike feeling which is not surprising since it set in when I was very little. It's time to take another look at my inheritance through grown-up eyes and to see if it changes my perspective on who I am. I've never been interested in history, thought that ancestors were irrelevant— until I discovered the man who designed the vest I'm wearing.

'No signs of an arrival yet then, Jenn?'

'No, but I'm sure it won't be long. And we really wanted to come out and encourage you on your way. But let's not hold you up— keep going. By the way, you look good in that white and red vest. And matching shorts and socks. Never seen you so coordinated.'

After a quick photo, I trot off downhill alongside a stand of sterile forestry pines, all straight edges and regimented rows. The residents of Bronze Age Threlkeld would never have seen trees arranged like that; they might be as bewildering to them as the internet. After I'm past the forestry, it's a mile or two on the little tarmac road downhill to Dockray. A big brown horse with a white blaze comes to the edge of its field to say hello over the fence, with its comforting warm breath blowing from huge trumpet nostrils. My back is hurting, running downhill on tarmac. I was in road shoes between home and St John's, then I changed into trail shoes for this section, and soon I'll be putting on fell shoes. That's something to look forward to.

Is It Serious?

Eee, will you giv us a hand wi the dishus pet?
There seems to be a lorra washin-up tunite.
Anyway, that lad ye seeing, is it serious?
I mean, well, yunno, wu divunt want any
unwanted surprises—de wu?

Well anyway pet, tak ya time—
that's my advice.
Ye divunt want te
marry the wrong bloke.

Did ye say yuv done yu homework?
You'll be alright, an intelligent girl like you.
But divunt,   yunno   get shoved into owt
yu divunt want. An,   yunno,   tak precautions.

Anyway, eee, that tea towel's manky
gerra clean un out.
Ye should marry a bloke,   yunno,   well
At least yu fancy im.

I mean I love you bairns but
when ee forces uz,
big fat belly pushin uz down
Eee, the pain.   Never mind.

Why havant yu wrung that dishcloth oot?
Get to sleep early tonight pet
before ee cumzin.   Mind,
wuv had a nice chat—
Havant wu?

3 *Lucky*

Dockray   Gowbarrow
              Fell   Swinburn Park

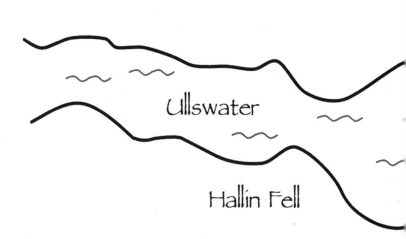

Ullswater

Hallin Fell

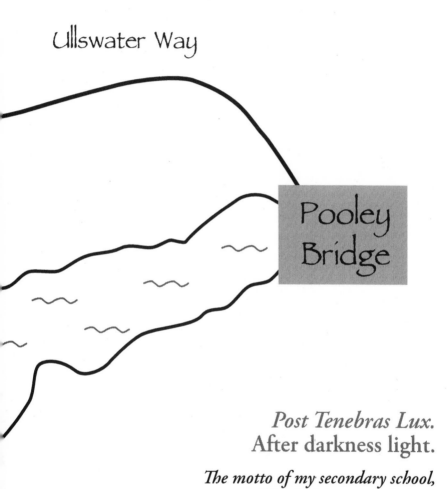

Ullswater Way

Pooley
Bridge

Post Tenebras Lux.
After darkness light.

The motto of my secondary school,
'The Bede', in Sunderland

'Join the army? Don't be ridiculous. You're far too intelligent for that.'

'No, it's the only option. I've got it all organised, filled in the forms and waiting for the medical.'

After my O-level exams at sixteen I was handing back my books to our physics teacher, baldy-headed Mr Faraday. I'd known him for three years and hated every minute of my time in his class. He seemed aloof and irrelevant, and nothing he tried to teach us seemed to have anything to do with the world we recognised. One day we were doing an experiment designed to show the expansion of metals by heat and my friend, Billy Henderson, was totally lost, sitting there clueless, not carrying out any instructions, so he got summoned to the front.

'Come here Henderson, put your hand out.'

Billy screamed and pulled away as Mr Faraday placed a hot metal rod across his palm. Some of us were shocked and hated Mr Faraday, but most of the class just laughed at Billy. After the bell went, I walked home with Billy; and the next day he came in trying to hide the bandage on his hand.

The day we started on electromagnetism really broke the deal with Mr Faraday and me. What the hell is electromagnetism and why does it have a spectrum? We might as well been studying witchcraft as far as I was concerned. So, when I went back into school to get my results and hand back the physics textbook, his concern for me came as a shock. I was sitting on a stool in his 'prep room' where the bench was completely covered with bits of wires and weird-looking stuff— silver globes and magnets and little screens which you couldn't watch the telly on. Wearing trainers, jeans and a Simon shirt, de rigueur 70s teenage fashion, I wasn't afraid of Mr Faraday—I was no longer a uniformed inmate; from then on, I had decided I would be the boss of me. Then he set to, giving me a pep-talk and persuading me that he would help me to apply for a grant to stay at school and do A-levels. He did get me thinking. What was so bad about staying at our house now that Dad was gone? A lot of the time, Mam wasn't even there. If I had a bit of money, it could work out fine. I could cope with it, couldn't I, for the sake of a future?

While changing into my fell shoes in the tiny riverside car park in Dockray and quaffing another mug of tea (courtesy of Mandy), I am met with a big smile by Nordic Nics, a woman I first met a couple of years ago at BBC Radio Cumbria. During the programme she taught me the Nordic walking technique, with poles, in the confines of the studio. We had both been asked to appear on *The Great Outdoors Show* and it was one of those wonderful chance encounters where you connect with someone straight away.

We have since shared many a long fell run together, most memor-ably one winter morning bathing in the sunrise on Blencathra, the fells covered in deep pristine snow and a golden light reflecting from all the tiny airborne crystals. It wasn't just the sun that was golden but the whole air. I want to say we were like a pair of floating angels in some Renaissance painting but we were much more alive than that. We were cold and bright and golden and I don't believe there can be any vision of heaven to rival such a winter morning on Blencathra with a friend.

I'm happy alone in the mountains, I even need to be up there alone at times. But for all the lonely hours I spend trotting about and musing, at times there's a little sadness if something astonishingly beautiful is unfolding and I have no companion to share it with. I wonder about that lonely feeling; is it that being out alone in big spaces is counter to the highly evolved human need to be in a group? It's dangerous to be separated from the protection of the tribe—there's safety in numbers. But it feels like more than a utilitarian need for security to want to share the enormous beauty of the fells. To set off in deep cold and dark, with head-torch light glinting on snow, to work hard up to a summit while the sun rises, to stand astonished together, in airborne gold. What that feels like, and what it means to share it, goes way beyond the need for safety. Heaven is not a lonely place.

Being a native of the Ullswater Valley, Nics is keen to join me for this section of my journey. She understands this is a special run for me, and I guess her coming to join me for a few miles is a validation of that understanding. We are already laughing as we leave the road and head up towards Gowbarrow Fell—my only *summit* of this whole pilgrimage. Not a big hill by Lake District standards, at just over one and a half thousand feet, but a lovely hill by my standards because of its panoramic view over Ullswater. After the Coach Road and the tarmac, it is a pleasure to be running up a fell on a steep muddy path punctuated by rocks. Using my hips and thigh muscles, judging the most efficient way of negotiating every step, each one different from the last. Up and up. We run steadily—balance, cadence and stride constantly changing.

Apparently Gowbarrow Fell means 'Windy Hill' in old Norse. Which is funny because by the time we get to the summit trig point, with its National Trust plaque denoting ownership of the fell, the wind seems to be dying down. We take a few minutes to enjoy the place. It's not sunny but the day is warming up, with a little patch of blue sky chinking through the fluffy clouds as white horses gallop across the surface of the lake.

This is a curated landscape. I wonder what the Norse folk, who came here little more than a thousand years ago, bringers of the nibbling Herdwick sheep, would make of the place in its denuded state. Perhaps they would say they never meant the sheep to take over, or for people to get paid by the state to destroy valuable habitat. The devastation of the English countryside by twentieth-century agricultural policies is all too easy to criticise in hindsight. But more optimistically, the strategy here in Cumbria is changing. Just down the valley from Gowbarrow Fell, near Patterdale, there is a re-wiggling project, rectifying the damaging straightening out of the watercourse. Liberating the living river from its manmade straitjacket is providing better habitat and reducing flood risk downstream. Learning from our mistakes, changing our minds and adapting—isn't Homo sapiens supposed to be good at all that?

And the couple who have recently inherited Gowbarrow Farm, Claire and Sam Beaumont, are putting into practice a new vision of farming, where food production, human and animal health and biodiversity are all nurtured together. Their practice of regenerative farming involves cattle which live outside, and pigs that forage, but no flock of sheep like Claire's grandfather kept. The idea of large herbivores living in a woodland ecosystem and yielding food is about as *natural* as it's possible to get. But the link between soil and trees and habitat and food has been broken for so long that what Claire and Sam are doing is now seen as *pioneering*. It's also more profitable than carrying on with sheep farming, which largely depends on government subsidies. The land under their watch is convalescing, the soil is improving and the species list is growing. Their meadows are not cut for silage—and curlews have returned.

The countryside is still able to heal when one invasive species of ape alters its behaviour.

Looking eastwards from Gowbarrow Fell summit, we can see beyond the edge of Cumbria to the Pennines. Gateshead seems like a mythical place, way beyond the eastern horizon. Another world. I bring my gaze back to the lake, which feels like it must always have been here, and yet a mere twelve thousand years ago it was still a glacier. Gradually, as things warmed up and woodlands became established, exotic creatures moved in, along with human hunters. Elk, reindeer, bears and wolves roamed the slopes of Gowbarrow Fell. Nothing stays the same in ecology; there is always flux. And although Sam and Claire's work won't bring back the bears and wolves and elk, Gowbarrow is an oasis of hope in our current epoch of crisis.

Nics and I both love running down rough fells and we take off down the hillside, lightly landing on the fronts of our feet, half flying, in a kind of dance which fully absorbs our concentration. The art of downhill fellrunning is the ultimate mindfulness training.

Sunderland Council came up trumps with my grant to go to sixth form, and I opened my first bank account to receive the cheque. From Jopling's Department Store, I bought myself a brand-new school blazer, a dark inky blue with a silver phoenix, our school emblem, embroidered intricately on the breast pocket. I had only ever had a second-hand nylon blazer with a roughly sewn-on badge before and it was never the right colour because Mam got cast-offs from the kids on our estate who went to a different school and wore a paler blue. My new woollen blazer felt warm, soft and substantial. I got it slightly big to help hide the curve in my back. There was something wrong with my back—most people called it slouching, though I really couldn't help it. But it was 1980 and I was a sixth-former with a posh blue blazer and determined to make the most of life.

1980 was all about Margaret Thatcher and Adam Ant. The age of free enterprise and opportunity, when, in theory, anyone could get rich if they worked hard enough. Competition bred success— this was the law of nature. Thatcher's assertion, 'There's no such thing as society', and reassertion of St Paul's diktat—'If a man shall not work, he shall not eat'—did not go down well in all quarters and most of the adults in our street were on the dole. To supplement my grant, I had a job at Presto's supermarket, a two-mile walk from our house. It was friendly, the money was good, and shifts were only eight hours on a Saturday and three hours on a couple of evenings. A favourite job was stacking the white sliced loaves because, even in their plastic coats, they had a sort of warm comforting smell and I usually spent 30p of my wages to bring one home for toast. It gave me great satisfaction to keep up with the price of everything, and it made my line at the checkout run down the fastest at busy times on Saturday mornings. Every item had to be rung up on an old-fashioned till and I took pride in being good at it. The price of sugar needed checking every week. For some reason, sugar was always going up and down.

School was full of promise but at the same time angsty and tricky. Chemistry was a big class—all boys, as I recall, except me and Ann from primary school, who according to our teacher were there to prove that girls couldn't do chemistry. Maths was relaxed and quirky. We hardly ever understood it, but when we did it was oddly wonderful. Life, though, was based in our biology class. We had our own den, the biology common room, where no teacher ever dared to enter. It was across the corridor from the lab and was just for us sixth-form biologists. Squeezed up on stools together, we would work, chat, and take turns to go down the chip shop for cheese and onion pasties at lunchtime. If one of us had no money, someone else would lend it and get paid back later. And I wonder if that could ever happen now—a bunch of kids from different worlds, some with professional parents and others scraping through poverty?

We were a kind of team. We helped each other, respected each other, and tolerated each other's differences. Some liked Brian Ferry but I preferred Bob Geldof. Most of us liked the local hero Sting and almost everyone loved the Rolling Stones. A couple of the lads were in the army cadets and a bunch of us were in CND. I'd changed my mind about the army. We would swap ideas for homework projects and go round to each other's houses to watch science programmes on BBC2. Romances would start and finish and start again or reconfigure. Some of us would get in trouble for not doing our homework or wearing the wrong clothes.

We'd often get drunk but usually in our own time, and it was only me who disgraced myself by being totally plastered on a field trip and throwing up in the minibus. I almost got thrown out for that. In the crudest terms you could say it had been a *cry for help*. Doing menial lab cleaning after school and being on a strict warning wasn't exactly the type of attention I was after. Yet I have to hand it to my impenetrable teachers, because it, sort of, worked. I tried to cajole myself not to drink so much and to do more schoolwork. I worried I might not be able to pass my exams, which everything depended on—they would be my passport out of Sunderland. But in the den of our biology common room, anxieties were calmed and dramas were played down. Problems were listened to, and plans were hatched. My biology class was my first tribe. They had my bent back and they brought out the best in me.

I often had our house to myself as Mam was mostly with her new fella. Tom was a contrast to our dad, who finally found another woman to service his needs and left when I was fifteen. Mam chose well this time round. Tom was quietly spoken, neatly dressed, and fun. He owned a nice house and had a car and a touring caravan, and he and Mam would often be off enjoying themselves on trips all round the UK. I was happy for her, and happy for the peace. When she was at home, the floorboard outside my bedroom would creak and I'd simmer with anger at the invasion as she burst through the door. Why couldn't she leave me alone? Just because she had fucked up most of her life didn't mean I had to do the same. I needed these A-levels.

'Mam! I'm trying to work.'

'Never mind that. That Sheila up the road who was in your class has just had a bairn, ee canny little thing. Du yu think you'll have bairns, pet? I mean not yet though, not like that Sheila, not even married. Once yu've got a nice bloke and got settled. Mind, I didn't like that lad yu were out with last week—never said a word when he came in. Yu told me he worked at the pit, but my friend said he's on the dole. Anyway, are yu cumin down for yu tea, then wu can put the telly on? Leave that book stuff now pet. Yu know what they say—all work and no play makes Jack a dull boy.'

Mam could talk about nothing for hours and demanded my full attention. But when she was out, it wasn't always easy to concentrate either. I often felt the familiar dread in my guts, a cold numb feeling, an inner knowing that she was right. Trying wouldn't change who I was meant to be. I was fooling myself if I thought my life would any different to hers. I was terrified that I would never escape, just work in Presto's and get pregnant. I went out with older men because they had money and cars and maybe …. yes, oh so pathetically, maybe there would be a cottage with roses round the door and someone who would take care of me. Too much reading *Pygmalion* in English lessons. I was careful to pop the little yellow contraceptive pills out of their foil packets and swallow them on the correct days. I had no idea how to use a condom and hoped the pill would work. I thought only gays got diseases, didn't they? To reduce my fears to tolerable, I would either get drunk or do something else to steady my soul—I would go for a run.

At times when I could concentrate, I was utterly enchanted by biology, and this fascination has never left me. Mam thought if I wanted to do something clever then I should aim to be a teacher, but I told her I was interested in plants and wanted to be a gardener. I wasn't serious, but the suggestion infuriated her, as I knew it would.

'Our Julie! That's not a woman's job, don't be stupid!'

What I really wanted was to be like one of those important biologists that our teacher Mrs Colclough taught us about, when she introduced a new topic through a new character in the story of knowledge. We learnt about important scientists, such as Carl Linnaeus who invented a system of taxonomy, for categorising and classifying living things; Louis Pasteur who discovered that microscopic life did not arise on its own but always came from the reproduction of other life; and the Austrian monk Gregor Mendel who, through his work with peas, discovered how genetic traits were inherited.

We also learnt about Edward Jenner who invented vaccination against smallpox; but no mention was made of Lady Mary Wortley Montagu who had introduced the practice to the West following her travels in Turkey several decades earlier. Although we learnt about the importance of symbiotic relationships in ecology, where creatures work together, such as that between the algae and fungi which constitute lichen, we never heard about the Cumbrian sheep farmer, Beatrix Potter, who had been a pioneer in that field. We learnt about Watson and Crick and the discovery of DNA but the biggest unsung hero of them all, Rosalind Franklin, whose work theirs had depended on, and which some say they stole, was never mentioned. The history of biology was male and white. But the future? Well, I thought the future could be different, despite my mam's dogmatic ideas about women and work.

The lynchpin of the whole story of the science of life, as we understood it, was the famous and brilliant, if sometimes misogynistic, Charles Darwin. Survival of the fittest—that was the law of nature championed by Darwin in his model of evolution by natural selection. Creatures who were fit and strong and successful survived to pass on their traits. Weaker specimens failed to reproduce and so their traits died out. Our first female prime minister, the Iron Lady of 1980s politics, believed that competition was vital for society to advance. But although the science behind Darwinism is solid, something about the whole thing wasn't quite adding up for me. How come I could get good grades and nurture high ambitions when my parents seemed so hopeless? How come I needed the help of a left-wing council to get an education? If the main purpose of my life was to pass on my genes, how come the thought of having kids filled me with horror? Mr Darwin and the Iron Lady—I realised their ideas were related and this was perplexing. As a good biology student, I respected Darwin as a genius; as a good little Mackem, I considered Thatcher to be the devil incarnate.

The steep downhill dance from Gowbarrow Fell is all too brief as the path continues more gently, winding down beside a drystone wall. Knowing that this run is partly an attempt to reflect on my ancestry, Nics is telling me about her family and how her elders spent a lot of time in a house in the village of Mardale Green in the next valley, east of Ullswater. After the construction of a huge dam, the village was flooded in the 1930s to provide a water supply for the ever-thirstier metropolis of Manchester. In exceptionally dry weather the usually submerged settlement, including a bridge and the remains of the church, can be seen emerging from the water. Nics' ancestors have lived round these parts for a long time but—like the houses of Mardale Green—many of their stories also remain submerged.

Nics and I are trotting easily along the well-made path of the Ullswater Way. It's not wide enough to run side by side but the wind is now just a breeze and it's easy to chat as I follow on behind her. There's no need to check the map, as Nics knows the place intimately. We talk about why we run, what got us into it and why we continue. For both of us, it is about connection, with our bodily selves and with the extraordinary place in which we live. Running brings an awareness of the body, of muscle and energy and heartbeat, an awareness of ourselves as living animals. Running in a place like this, absorbing the exhaled breath of trees and noticing every root and patch of boggy ground under our feet, makes us feel that we ourselves have grown out of the earth. The path levels off as it enters a plantation of pines at Swinburn Park, the designation 'Park' giving a clue that aristocrats hunted deer here, in medieval times. Just through the gate I notice a little stone sculpture in the shape of a sheep's horn with the word 'yan' engraved in the stone.

We still have a half view of the lake filtered through the trees on our right and the running is gentle and easy. Soon everything opens up to a tremendous panorama because the hillside below us has been felled in recent years. The fully grown crop of wood, which may now be gracing homes as IKEA furniture or the like, has been replaced with miniature Christmas trees, not much higher than my knee. Our path is a terrace looking out over the lake; and directly over the water there's a great view of Hallin Fell, which was my lunchtime run for the four years I worked at Howtown Outdoor Centre in my early twenties. I could get up and down in half an hour and still have time for a good lunch, including a substantial pudding, courtesy of the wonderful Hilda who ran the Centre's kitchen. I somehow feel surprised to see Hallin Fell—I had almost forgotten it was there. I haven't thought about those years for a long time and begin to feel nostalgic. Usually, I only think about the run I'm doing now or runs I'm planning in the future, but seeing Hallin Fell snuggled in the crook of Ullswater is making me reflect that I've been running for a long time and that running is the thing I have always relied on, to keep me connected to the world and to myself.

Running has brought me immeasurable rewards; and over the years the reasons I run and the way I run have shifted. For a while I was addicted to the buzz of racing. The first time I ever won was in a ten-kilometre road race. I liked winnning. No—I loved winning, especially when it was close and I had to give every ounce of me to achieve it. I won a ten-mile road race once because I ran right behind my competitor, fighting to keep pace and using her to protect me from the headwind, until less than a mile from the end. Then, when I sensed her weakening slightly, and when I felt the end was close enough for me to make it and not slow down, I got past. And I might as well have been running for my life; running as if the one who would win would be the only one to survive. Five minutes later, my rival and I would be having a friendly chat over plastic cups of weak orange squash and home-made sandwiches and cake.

Running is a bit like acting—an artistic expression. Art and sport are both ways of playing things out, creating some new vision of oneself and of the world. It's easy to see why running feels good in general but why should racing and winning feel good? Is it an inbuilt need to express our individual egos and crush the opposition? Is it born of ancient hunting instincts, wanting to be the one to catch the prey? You can dream up all sorts of psychological theories but anybody who has been closely involved with a running community will know that racing at its best is about exactly that—community. When we celebrate the winner, we celebrate the race itself, and it inspires all of us. Of course it feels good to be the one getting the approval and attention in that moment. For me it's more to do with the happiness of being at the heart of things than any deep-seated instinctive drive to beat other people. I'd like to think the foot races I take part in are somehow akin to a communal bodily work of art, rather than a contest. In running races I need my competitors and they need me. Competition can be collaboration, at least in sport. The friend I outran in the ten-mile race went on to beat me many times over.

As Nics and I get further along this glorious terrace above Ullswater, tall trees appear again on our right and close off the view. The light is strange and the lower branches of the pines are covered in thick lurid green moss, like the antlers of a young deer still covered in fur. For a few minutes we run past these otherworldly trees and the green of the moss is jarring and garish. Even though they were planted by humans, nature still creates an ecosystem. A woodland is, above all, a multicultural community of plants and fungi, lichens and bacteria. And the trees communicate with each other and protect each other and depend on each other. Life is not a simple matter of competition. Mr Darwin understood much of this but it's always the 'survival of the fittest' headline that gets heard and makes it into popular culture and school textbooks. Before we emerge from the trees, on the edge of the wood, is a group of sturdy trunked birch which are probably as old as many generations of commercial timber. Under them is another sheep horn sculpture and this one says 'tyan'. And a bit further on, just near another gate, is a third which says 'tethera'.

'What are these about, Nics?'

'They are the Herdwick Stones. *Yan* is one, *tyan* is two, *tethera* is three. Its old Norse or something and the stones are by a local sculptor, Charlotte Ruse, in celebration of shepherding culture.'

'Why, yan, tyan, tethera, though?'

'It's the counting system they would have used for counting the Herdwicks. It goes up to twenty and then they move a stone from one pocket to another and start back at yan. Five stones is a hundred sheep.'

We run on through some fields, cross a little road and more fields, to the hamlet of Bennethead. Nics has moved on from sheep and is telling me about the benefits of nose breathing and I am intrigued. She says if you can train yourself to keep your mouth closed and inhale only through your nose it has lots of health benefits. It makes the breathing muscles fitter and helps you run much more efficiently.

'Surprised you don't know about this Jules, with you being a doctor.'

'Well Nics, it's actually very suprising—all the things doctors haven't got a clue about.'

I'm well entertained as we run on through more fields and woods and take a labyrinth of paths down through a caravan park and onto the lakeshore road.

'I can't believe your luck about the bridge; it was closed all last week and yesterday. I was thinking about what we would do if was still shut. It would have added miles onto your route to go round.'

Pooley's stone bridge, built in 1764, was destroyed in the devastating Storm Desmond in 2015. The replacement is to be Britain's first stainless-steel road bridge and to my eye it's looking good. The single steel span is much sleeker than the beautiful old two-arch stone construction, but it's of its time and I like it. There was a pedestrian walkway over the river during the building phase, but for the final stage the walkway had to be closed. A fact which I was blissfully unaware of until I got a text message from Nics last night.

'The Bridge will be open! Been closed all week but opening in the morning.'

And just on the other side, parked in the middle of the bustling village, is Mandy. Nics is right—I'm one lucky woman. What if I hadn't met Mandy all those years ago and fallen in love? What if she hadn't had the endless patience to stick with me? What if baldy Mr Faraday hadn't diverted me from the army? Above all, what if I'd never started running? I wonder if I'd even be alive, let alone soaking up friendship and love and sunshine.

'Here's a mug of tea. Do you want soup as well? Are you changing back to trail shoes or keeping those on?'

Mandy has everything I might need or want to hand. Lucky doesn't cover it.

Do the Maths

Mostly we learned about wounds because you rarely missed
the target. You Sir—the Olympic thrower of the blackboard rubber.
By miles our most outstanding weapons were our words.
Our etched and gum-stuck desk lids were useless shields.
We sang Donny Osmond in harmony out of defiance.
We knew how to solve your quadratic equations all the time
until the twelfth of never, until the poets are out of rhyme.
And you never knew how good we could be at kicking
balls because girls were never allowed to play footy.

Teachers should not throw hard objects.
Teachers should not draw pupil's blood.

Balls!—because girls were never allowed to play footy.
And you never knew how good we could be at kicking
until the twelfth of never. Until the poets were out of rhyme
we knew how to solve your quadratic equations every time.
We sang Donny Osmond in harmony out of defiance.
Our etched and gum-stuck desk lids were useless shields.
By miles—our most outstanding defences were our words
the target—you Sir!—the Olympic thrower of the blackboard rubber.
Mostly we learned about woundings because we rarely missed.

4 Survival of the Fittest

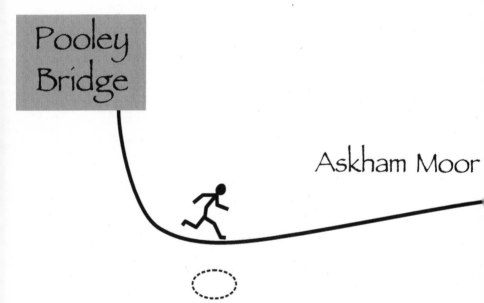

Pooley Bridge

Askham Moor

The Cockpit

I consider myself fortunate to have been able to develop my running ability when so many others can only sit and wonder what they might have been able to achieve.

Sir Brendan Foster

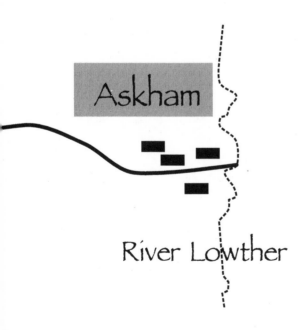

S omething different had been happening in the spring of 1981 —for the first time I'd noticed the odd person out in the streets, going for a run. Seeing people going for a run was something very new. Many of them were preparing for the big event, 28th June, hyped up in the local papers on the regional TV news, the first ever Great North Run. I watched the race on the telly at home, intrigued. But I was only an onlooker. This didn't have anything to do with me—or so I thought. I had no idea of the seismic importance, to me, of what was about to take place that day.

The cameras panned across the crowd as the seconds ticked down, and muscles twitched and legs shuffled on the start line while butterflies fluttered in stomachs. Even on the telly I could almost smell the embrocation and anticipation which filled the air. There was none of the usual traffic noise in Newcastle city centre as even the city's motorway was closed for race day. The buzz was building as runners checked their shoelaces and discarded the bin bags they had been wearing over their vests to keep warm before the start. The time had come, and the front runners lent forward into readiness. The cannon boomed, the runners surged, and a new era of people's running burst forth.

Up to the early 1980s, long-distance running in the UK had been the preserve of a small crew of elite athletes. Even the biggest races would have hundreds not thousands of entrants. But in March 1981 the first London Marathon had just over 6,000 runners and three months later, on that sunny morning in June, emotion infused the bright-blue Tyneside sky as 12,264 people gathered close together. One tribe with a single focus. And most of them had never done anything like this before. Most of them were about to run further than they had ever run, and they were starting a kind of running revolution, the scale of which was unimaginable at the time. Amid the rising heart rates and the rising energy, there were wisecracks, jokes and smiles. Nerves cloaked in Geordie camaraderie. Sporting their tight shorts, mid-calf socks, and stripey sweatbands, very few of the runners knew what to expect. At the end of their thirteen and a little bit miles, when 12,000 sweaty pairs of feet crossed the line, they were not at the finish, they were at the start of something. They were starting a revival in the ancient human instinct to run.

The first ever Great North Run half marathon had been advertised as a local fun run by the Gateshead Olympian, Brendan Foster. His ambition was to get people enthused about running and thought maybe three or four thousand could be encouraged to take part. His former Gateshead Harriers coach, Stan Long, devised a fourteen-week training programme for the public to follow. Sponsorship was encouraged to raise a million pounds for a scanner for a local hospital to aid cancer diagnosis. BBC Look North got involved and Brendan's hopes to get Tynesiders out running were massively exceeded. Brendan ran the race in an hour and nine minutes; despite being retired from running, he led by example. The England football captain Kevin Keegan, who had played for both Newcastle and Sunderland, ran it in a half red-and-white and half black-and-white shirt, but the shoes were obviously not suitable as he got terrible blisters. A boy of seventeen from Gateshead, in a full-length leg plaster, did it on crutches. A blind woman who was new to running did it with her guide dog. Several wheelchair athletes competed. A quarter of a million people came to cheer— the biggest running celebration in the world. And on the whole, it wasn't about competition; it was about participation. Running together as a group, encouraging each other to keep going. What is the collective noun for runners? A field, a pack, a tribe, a happiness?

After my pit-stop in sunny Pooley Bridge and saying goodbye to Nics, I jog slowly up the lane which leads to Askham Moor. I am on my own again now; and although I have not run this exact route before, the land is familiar from the years I spent at Howtown Outdoor Education Centre, just along the shores of Ullswater. In my early twenties I was employed there to run courses for teenagers, the purposes of which were obvious but difficult to define. Climbing, fell walking, scrambling, swimming, orienteering, kayaking, canoeing, sailing and windsurfing were all on the agenda.

I would come with walking groups from the centre up here onto Askham Moor. It's a great place to teach kids about maps and how to navigate. There are all kinds of peculiar little features which hint that humans have been on this land for a very long time. One of the oddities on the map which intrigued my pupils was 'The Cockpit'. I would set them off to use their compasses to find it, and when they got there, to explore and come back to tell a story about it. What was it? Why was it there? What did they think might have happened there? They did not know beforehand what to expect from The Cockpit, and some thought it would turn out to be the remains of a crashed aircraft.

In fact, it is a Neolithic stone circle surrounded by burial mounds and ancient earthworks. When you are only thirteen, 3,000 years makes no sense at all. The stories my students told often involved time travel to the future or the past. Without knowing anything of the history, my young narrators picked up on a vibe. Pretty much every story they told involved some kind of magic ritual, even though they didn't *believe* in the supernatural. Except one set of stories, from a group of kids from a strict Catholic school, which were quite different. They said The Cockpit was a natural rock formation, it was geology, and it was made by God not by humans. I think they were the only ones who really believed in their own story. The others suspended their disbelief, just to have some fun with their imaginings and begin to get under the skin of the thing we call time.

I'm enjoying the steady uphill running on easy grass paths and the day is really warm now. It's more like summer than late September, and the sky is a totally uncompromising postcard blue. Gaining height, the stone circle of The Cockpit comes into view a few hundred yards to my right although the stones are diminutive in comparison to those at Castlerigg.

On the skyline ahead is a stand of pines inside a wall. They are forestry-planted pines, but a bit more tree-like than the sardine-packed stand above Dockray, with room for their branches to spread a little. Maybe some Ents are amongst them. And up by the wall there's a group of feral fell ponies with Kate Bush hairdos. These horses also came with the Vikings, or so the story goes. Askham Moor always feels like an old place to me, even on a bright new day like today. I ran across the moor in the pitch dark once, on the winter solstice, and never dared to look behind me. Now in the sunshine it makes me smile to recollect William Wordsworth's description of seeing a hare when he was taking a walk up here one morning.

All things that love the sun are out of doors;

The sky rejoices in the morning's birth;

The grass is bright with raindrops;—on the moors

The hare is running races in her mirth;

And with her feet she from the plashy earth

Raises a mist, that, glittering in the sun,

Runs with her all the way, wherever she doth run.

I want to be like the hare and run races in my mirth. And it's lovely easy running underfoot and although I am alone, I feel accompanied, as my feet enjoy the 'plashy earth'.

Eventually the moor gives way to a stony track and down to the road into Askham village. Near the village shop I catch up with a bloke running, but I can't just whisk by with a passing 'Hi' as our speeds are too well matched not to chat a little so I venture a greeting.

'Lovely day.'

'Beautiful isn't it. Are you going far?'

I hesitate a moment not wanting to have to explain myself—what can I say?

'Yeah, quite a way, I'm running to Gateshead. Started from Keswick this morning.'

'Oh right. Well, enjoy yourself. I'm parked just here. See ya.'

Relieved not to be questioned further, considering Gateshead is still well over seventy miles away, making my comment seem a bit bizarre, I run on down the hill to the idyllic spot by the River Lowther where Mandy is parked. Time for the yoga mat to come out onto the grass so I can do some stretches. The downhill on steep tarmac through the village has taken its toll and now, with my back hurting, I'm crampy and tired. And what's coming next will be a challenge. It's road shoe time again.

In sixth form, nothing ever happened during 'form time', as we would all be strewn across the benches of darkly stained wood, fighting our teenage circadian rhythms, sometimes accidentally gassing ourselves by snoozing and leaning on the Bunsen burner taps. The lab smelt different from the chalky classrooms—not just tank and the stale sawdust of the mouse cage. Linda was usually late. She never got any sleep because her parents had loud arguments all night long. We had a connection, Linda and me. Of course, we had no language, no words to describe the sickening void that living in a domestic war zone creates in a girl's soul. But we recognised each other, in our understated, play down the drama, pre-social-media age. Sometimes she would arrive red-eyed and on the way to first lesson would struggle to contain her tears.

All I could say was: 'Try and pretend you're somewhere else. It won't last forever. My dad left two years ago. The bastard. Before that, nobody slept for years. You're better than them Linda, you'll be alright. Anyway, come round ours any time. When me mam's out, it's dead quiet.'

For myself I thought my only chance was to pass some exams, but Linda had more imagination. One morning she turned up on time wearing the race T-shirt of the first ever Great North Run over her school shirt. The T-shirt was white with blue writing. Under Linda's blazer it didn't stand out straight away, until she perched on a lab stool, shed the blazer and stuck her chest out, grinning. We, her friends, thought this was brilliant. There were smiles, pats on the back (nobody hugged in 1981) and incredulous questions about how she had managed it.

Mrs Colclough was not impressed: 'Get that off. You know what uniform is.'

I was stunned by this heartless diktat. My friend had become a hero and in her finest hour was cut down. Linda's grin, which had lit up the room, was swiftly extinguished by Mrs Colclough's pronouncement. If I had been the teacher, I would have had Linda up at the front of the class celebrating. I don't blame our teacher, she was a good person in so many ways, but she would never let the rules slip. There were things you could share with teachers and things you couldn't. Our experience was that teachers taught us subjects and, for reasons only they knew, they did not lift the lids on the lives of kids like us. Girls like us. There was no point saying anything to Mrs Colclough about what Linda's triumph meant, even if we'd had the words, but we clubbed together to buy Linda a Cadbury's Curly-Wurly and a bottle of Blue Nun at lunchtime.

Linda had inherited the ability to run, as most of us have, because we are a species of hunter. Linda was not hunting for food but hunting for self-confidence, for connection, for hope. I begin to wonder what has happened to her in the forty years since we last met; and it's only now that I begin to understand how much I owe her.

I can't say exactly how it started, but soon after Linda's trail blazing, it just started. Our council house was on the edge of an estate and within a few minutes of running I could be through the pack of dogs roaming free at the end of our street and down a farm lane, through a park, along a road to a hill beside the new outdoor dry ski slope on the site of a closed-down coal mine. I started going running, aimlessly and on my own. It was like the junior school playground feeling but much better. There were no limits. I could run as fast and as far as I wanted to, and it had nothing to do with anyone except me. It had no purpose, no plan, no objective. It just felt good and most of the time, good was not how I felt.

As I came back onto the Thorney Close council estate I'd often be greeted by shouts of 'get those knees up' and other wisecracks from young kids circling like vultures on their Chopper bikes. Dodging the dogs and their turds was always alarming and it puzzled me that some dogs had black shit, others brown and some even had white. Instinctively I felt there was something very disturbing about white shit. I knew from my studies that poo was brown because of bilirubin, a breakdown product of blood cells, which is secreted into the gut from the liver though bile. Perhaps I could ask Mrs Colclough about the dogs with white shit. Or perhaps not.

Now I have my own road half marathon to run between Askham
and my planned overnight stop. I used to love road running. I
loved the rhythm, the predictabilty, the trance-like pace of it. The
way you could go to the edge of yourself because all you had to
think about was the body, the legs, the feet, the breath, the chest,
the arms, the rhythm, the rhythm, the rhythm. Expending energy
at just the right rate. Sustaining the almost unsustainable. There's
something pure about road running, and something horrible
too—roads can be unforgiving, even for people with anatomically
well-built bodies. An x-ray of my thoracic spine reveals it to be
rounded like the arc of a wheel. Instead of rungs off the sides of a
ladder, my ribs are spokes converging onto the front of my chest.
The weightiest part of my body, my head, is too far forward. The
muscles of my behind—my lower back, arse and hamstrings—
have a big job on to pull my balance back so I don't fall over
forwards. And the more I ran the road, the tighter and more
contracted everything became, until road running was no longer a
pleasure. It's a regret, because—apart from the back pain—I was
naturally good at road running. I could have been really good at it.

I had looked at the map of east Cumbria—for hours and days,
and weeks and months. There was no getting past it. The only
feasible way to get out of the Lake District, over the mainline
railway and across the M6 into the Pennines was to do a good
chunk of road running. There were some other possibilities but
they were all worse. Some paths on the map were blocked or
hopelessly overgrown on the land. In a way it's ironic that because
of all the modern improvements in transport links it is no longer
easy to make certain journeys on foot. I don't wish myself back
into the Middle Ages. I enjoy being able to get to places quickly. A
week's holiday in the northwest of Scotland wouldn't be much use

if you had to get there on foot. There are times, though, when sitting in my car, I gaze out over England's green and grassy land and it just feels barren, stripped naked and flogged. The English countryside is an agricultural desert scattered with small oases where trees and remaing wildlife take refuge.

Preparing for this part of the run had been a trade-off between doing a small amount of flattish road training but not doing enough to cause me any damage. As well as my back problems, becoming very absorbed in fellrunning was also a factor in my falling out of love with road running. But then I had another type of fall which changed everything. On a Derbyshire gritstone edge one summer afternoon in 2018 there was not much more than ten feet between me and the ground. But a second later, while reaching over leftwards to a crack where I could place some protection to clip my rope into, I overstretched and slipped off, becoming sharply acquainted with a pointy rock that impacted my arse. Lying shaking in the heather, focussing on staying calm, breathing as best I could through the pain, I immediately knew I had fractured my pelvis. I just tried to keep still, keep breathing and wait for assistance. Mandy and another friend were with me and a kind passer-by also came to help.

The Edale Mountain Rescue team eventually arrived. They were gentle and respectful; I could not have been in better hands. I gritted my teeth through the torture of the pelvic brace for the stretcher lift and the helicopter flight to hospital. Bodily and emotionally relinquishing myself to strangers, no longer able to sustain myself without the care and skill of others. It was like being inside a forcefield of care, feeling protected and held. Until these brilliant volunteers passed me onto the professionals.

I tried to be patient with the medics in the hospital who did not listen to me, who did things to me without my consent, and who seemed to ignore every real need I had. They missed the fractured ribs and bleeding left lung—even though I told them I could feel the grind of the broken bones with every struggled breath. They gave me an injection of intravenous contrast for a scan without giving me any intravenous fluids, when I was severely dehydrated, and so almost poisoned my kidneys. They ignored my vomiting and pain. They ignored my requests for an ice pack for my hugely bruised and broken bottom. They asked me to walk without crutches when I almost fainted with the pain of doing it. They did not check the nerves in my lower body even though the fractures went all the way through the places where nerves make their exit from the spine.

Eventually my survival instinct prevailed and after twenty-four hours I just upped and left. I hobbled out of the hospital and onto the bed in our van so that Mandy could take me home. It was the longest walk of my life. I couldn't get into a wheelchair; it was two months before I could sit down, and crutches were not on offer. The next day my kind GP arranged for me to go to our local hospital fracture clinic and I was instructed to use crutches and not weight-bear for a few weeks until the pain settled.

Well okay, I thought—I'll just hobble about on crutches and get myself better. In my mind I gave it two or three months—I would be healed up by then. Except that over two years later I'm not. Bodies are remarkable regenerating miracles. But they are also books in which our stories are written and my pelvis is still telling the story of my fall. So I can't do much road running any more, which I don't much mind about most of the time. But I'll have to do some now, to get where I want to be. First I'll do some stretching and have a drink. This is a lovely spot down by the water's edge, beside the pink sandstone bridge of the River Lowther. The sun is out and the water is slow and serene. What's more there is a flat space for my yoga mat. It being a sunny Sunday, there are plenty of people out and about, enjoying walks and picnics, so I feel a bit self-conscious as I spend some time in 'child pose' and move onto 'pigeon pose' before doing some spinal twists. Then I sit for just a moment, and watch the water and enjoy my brew, but it would be unwise to rest for long and let my muscles cool. I adjust the laces of my seldom-worn road shoes.

'Right then Mandy. I'll be off.'

In Mrs Colclough's class we enthusiastically learnt about biology's poster boy, Charles Darwin, and not so respectfully about another bloke on the scene around the same time, a professor called Jean-Baptiste Lamarck. This Frenchman had some very queer ideas of how evolution worked, which were seen to be in direct conflict with Mr Darwin's. We all had a good old laugh at Lamarck. He must have been some kind of dunce, really. Every society has stories about how we and our world came into being. In modern western cultures some people still think that all species were made just as they are by a god, and others think life has changed throughout its history and evolved.

In our 1980s Northern English comprehensive, the god idea was laughed at too. We were scientists and we never encountered strange ideas such as 'intelligent design', the idea that things have evolved but 'under god's direction'. Science was our belief system and, in a much-expanded way, science still is my belief system. The idea that evolution happened was never questioned in our education, since it had been proven by irrefutable evidence. Darwin had done detailed work demonstrating how finches had evolved various-shaped beaks, adapting to different food sources. In London's moths, the darkest offspring survived because their colour best matched that of the pollution-tainted trees they inhabited, rendering them less likely to be seen and eaten. These offspring then passed on their dark wing colour and the pale forms died out in the city. These are observable examples of evolution, demonstrating that living creatures change in response to their environment. It is the mechanism of how the changes happen that Charles Darwin is credited with explaining.

This French bloke, Lamarck, had said things evolved by a process called 'the inheritance of acquired characteristics'. This meant that if a creature, such as a giraffe, could gain an advantage by acquiring a characteristic, such as a long neck to reach more nourishing vegetation, then it could stretch to make its neck longer and reach all those juicy leaves high up. All that sticking its neck out would cause its baby giraffes to have necks that were a bit longer. Mams and dads could improve themselves and, by some biological mechanism yet to be explained, their babies would also be biologically improved. That was Lamarck's theory of evolution by 'acquired characteristics'.

But Darwin said that wasn't how evolution worked most of the time. Dads who lifted a lot of pints down the pub would *not* have bairns with strong biceps. Darwin said creatures varied because of the mixing up of things passed on from their mams and dads, and also what was passed on just spontaneously changed a bit, by accident. Now and then a new ability or feature pops up in a creature by chance, and if that new thing helps survival, then that creature will survive and have lots of offspring. If the new thing is bad for survival, it will die out. This is the 'survival of the fittest model' or 'evolution by natural selection', where the environment selects the individuals most suited to it.

The important thing in Darwin's theory is that the fitness to survive and have babies depends on the mixing of inheritance from different parents, plus a little bit of new spontaneous variation. Darwin did not know that the inheritance happened through DNA and did not understand what made the new variation, but he observed it cropping up here and there and that it seemed to do so by chance. He realised parents did not pass on things that happened to themselves in their lives. The process of making new life involved a mingling of information from parents, along with a bit of new variation. It could be helpful or harmful variation and it seemed to be random. In contrast to Lamarck, Darwin said what made life evolve was not effort, it was chance.

Darwin was right and a visionary, and Lamarck was an idiot. That was the argument presented in our class and we were all convinced. (Geneticists wouldn't demonstrate that there was actually a bit of truth in Lamarck's ideas until we were almost into the twenty-first century. But that understanding was yet to come.) Even though we were teenagers and distracted by our own biological impulses, we all loved biology classes. No matter how tired, or anxious or in love we were, when we came into the lab and perched on our stools for a biology class we were motivated to learn because Mrs Colclough never gave a boring lesson. Sometimes she would have a bit of a freak-out when she told us the list of things on the syllabus we absolutely had to cover before the exams. How could we fit it all in? It was obvious that she loved it all as much as we did. And when we asked questions and got into more detail than we needed to, she couldn't help throwing herself into it and abandoning the syllabus. She made us feel excited about all this knowledge, that this was an evolving story and that we, an unlikely bunch of kids in our lab in Sunderland, were part of it. At times she would almost have us believing that we could be just like Mr Darwin—travelling to the Galapagos, going on journeys of discovery that would change the world.

On one field trip I did a survey of limpet shell shapes and found a correlation between shell shape and position on the rocks. The more exposed limpets had a different shape. Was this because they had pulled their own shell into a flatter shape by contracting their hanging-on-muscles or was it because the ones that had genetically inherited that shape were the ones that survived in the exposed places? Who knew? I devised an experiment to test the two hypotheses but ran into technical difficulties when I saw that the limpets I'd marked and moved—to test their ability to adapt—just moved themselves back to where they'd come from. Limpets have autonomy and I hadn't allowed for that in my experimental design.

My best work was an experiment with barnacles, measuring their feeding activity in a tank with no light and no tide. I got up every two hours around the clock for three days and nights. I expected they would just feed randomly as they no longer had cues from the environment but, surprisingly, they all fed at the same time, in synchrony with a tidal pattern which was no longer present in their world. They had something inside themselves which *knew* the tide tables and the time. How? I was sure that real scientists must have this stuff all worked out and the answer to that would be known. But it wasn't until 2017 that a Nobel Prize was awarded for the discovery of the biological mechanism that underpins circadian rhythms. Three scientists worked out that cells have genes which program their 'molecular clock'. Which makes me think I may have been onto something and wonder how many more sixth-form scientists are onto stuff right now?

I remember the barnacles experiment well because Mrs Colclough was a bit concerned about my own sleep pattern. But to her credit, she allowed me access to the lab at the field studies centre where we were staying at all times of the day and night. Perhaps she thought focussing on the project I had conjured up might help me stay sober. This was also the first time I remember doing any real statistics, figuring out what constitutes convincing evidence in science, or what the likelihood is that the results just happened as a fluke. If I am starting to sound like a nerd, it's nothing to the souls who really lost themselves in this type of research. Mr Darwin wrote several books on the subject of barnacles alone.

Choices

I was born in Sunderland on the 10th April 1964,
in the early hours of the morning before dawn.

What did you get for your Birthdays?

I got colouring crayons and Lego, and a pink teddy. I got shoes I loved;
a jumper I didn't like.
I always asked for books, but nobody gave me books.
One year I got an Easter egg with chocolates inside and I tried my very,
very best to make it
last.

I got drunk on my brother's home brewed beer. I got a stout clout round
the head.
I got a ringside seat at a soap opera where a man fucked his unwilling wife.

I got fear, cold and constant. I got secrets I could not keep.
I got fucked when I was still a child.
I always asked for a puppy but nobody gave me a puppy.

I got blood, and bones, and breath.
I got legs that can run fast.
I got eyes that I can keep open, and look, and see, and wonder.

I got the choice to speak or be silent.
The choice to listen and hear uncomfortable truths.
The choice to breathe or hold it, or freeze, or fight, or fly.
I got the choice to imagine, the choice to trust myself.
The choice to try to love.
I got choices.
It was a hell of a present.

5 A Touch of Gold

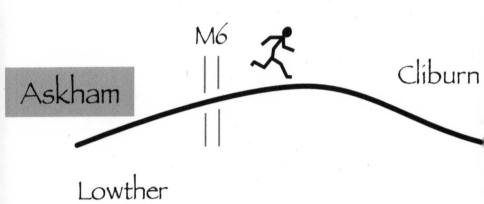

Askham

M6

Cliburn

Lowther
Castle

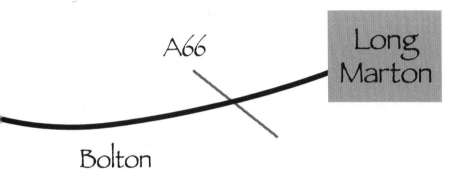

A66

Long Marton

Bolton

Every girl, no matter where she lives, deserves the opportunity to develop the promise inside of her.

Michelle Obama

It was a bone-freezing day in the winter of 1982/3; the air was still as a statue, as low shining sunshine flooded the university playing fields, all glinting with frost. Outside the sports centre I lined up in shorts and a vest, perked up by the zinging cold air on my skin. It's funny how when cold is really cold it almost becomes warming, like it switches on an inner energy. This wasn't an important race; it was only a bit of lunchtime fun. It was a relay, with four in a team, and I was last to go—the anchor. Our third runner was a redheaded rugby player, and it wouldn't be hard to see him coming. I jumped and jiggled about, blowing on my hands and swinging my arms, waiting for our guy to appear across the field. I was ridiculously nervous, and ridiculously cold. It was minus several degrees and the air had that fiery smell of ice, burning my nose with every breath.

It was only the second time in my life that I had dared to take part in an actual race of any sort. (The first was that ill-conceived adventure at a school's cross-country event years earlier.) Every year the staff and students of the Biology Department at York University formed teams and ran the 'Biology Relays'. A short course round the university fields, which was meant to forge bonds between staff and students and get everyone out of their labs. This year it was an 'ice-breaker' in more than one sense. The winter sun was huge and blinding, and a line of lanky poplar trees stood in a guard of honour along the edge of the course. It was as if King Midas had been for a jog around in front of us and touched everything. The university's box-like buildings, the sky, the trees—everything was golden, except the grass which was sparkling silver with frost crystals. A jewelled carpet for us to race on; only the footing was treacherous in normal road trainers, which was all I had to run in. My team-mate came gasping in and held out his hand to tag me for the off.

The course wasn't much more than a mile, short enough for adrenaline to do some powerful work. I sped round and managed to keep upright. My trainers seemed to be sticking to the grass okay, but it was hard to see the patches of pure ice with the blinding sun, and I had a few skates and near misses. I was running to my limit, breathing heavily, with the bite of the freeze in the back of my throat. I had passed a few runners but now there was no one ahead. Soon I was over the line. We had won! Claps and cheers and smiles and even some of the lecturers and professors who, to me, were the equivalents of living Darwins and Einsteins, shook my hand and said, 'Well done'. It was friendly and fun, and I was the fastest runner round the course, which surprised me. I wished I had brought my jumper from the changing room though and I jogged back to the sports centre almost as fast as I had raced, desperate to be first into the hot showers.

It was only a small thing to have done well in, but I liked all those friendly, 'Well done', 'Wow, you're a good runner Julie' comments after the relay, and the feeling that people would say good things to me because of a run. A run. I did like to run. But up until that lunchtime I had been embarrassed about it. Up until that lunch-time it was something I did early in the mornings, on the sly.

Another student was in the university cross-country team and was quick to recruit me. I soon signed up for more muddy and bracing outings but none that I remember were ever as cold. For days after the relay, I felt like someone had scrubbed the inside of my lungs with a Brillo pad. Going around the Biology Department you could tell who had run and put some effort in. Cough, cough, cough, and a reluctance to engage in too much conversation as the voice faded into a hoarse whisper after a few words and the cough would start again. My success made me smile though, and the Brillo-pad feeling wore off after a while, by which time I was a fully-fledged member of the university cross-country team with my first ever team vest which was pure black with a golden stripe around the chest and just the word 'YORK' in golden letters above the stripe.

Now I'm in the middle of the Indian summer's day as I set off up the steep road past Lowther Castle and leave the Lake District behind. The September afternoon is hot and I have approximately 13 miles of road running ahead of me. I break it down into smaller pieces in my mind and just think about it a bit at a time. The view from the bridge over the M6 is a contrast to the summit view from Gowbarrow Fell earlier this morning. The mesmerising buzz of traffic whizzing under the bridge, every vehicle containing a story, a journey, a reason to get from A to B. Restlessness is in our blood. I am trying to persuade myself the road run is good, the road can be enjoyable. Just try and tell the pain noise to turn down. Tune out of it. Like tuning out from the voice of a nagging mother.

Along the minor roads of the Eden Valley, I'm trying to find a steady pace, sometimes moving onto the grass verge to ease the impact. My whole physical experience of life has changed during my fifties. I can no longer rely on myself in the way I used to. First came prolapsed discs and damaged nerves. Because my thorax cannot move, the rest of my back took the excess load. Then there was menopause and I thought I would never emerge from the fog. Sometimes my thermo-regulation was so out of kilter I felt like I had the flu. I took to swallowing infusions of sage from the garden. It helped. To be helped by another species is a wonderful thing. I don't believe plants have benevolent intentions specifically towards me. They just evolved to be themselves but in doing so they support all aspects of my life. I respect them; depend upon them. But since the climbing accident, what I have needed more than anything is a dose of patience with myself. And I haven't been sure how to find it.

Unless I'm racing, I need some entertainment when road running; otherwise it's purgatory. I often go on mind journeys and things come to me that would not manifest themselves in any other situation. Running seems to allow ideas to flow in a way that doesn't happen otherwise; and hours can pass when I am absorbed in seemingly random mental chatter until, like spotting some pieces that fit in a jigsaw, I find something interesting that was buried within. When my body no longer feels fluid and at ease, I enjoy escaping into my own thoughts. I alternate between this state of being, existing as a disembodied intellect, with trying to tune into myself, adjusting my posture, relaxing, breathing better, seeking moments of feeling the flow of being a runner. This body awareness is good, helpful stuff. But it's hard to sustain and there is a voice of self-distrust within me whose volume is amplified by sensations of pain.

'You're only going to break yourself if you carry on. Stop. It's too much, you'll not be able to do it.'

I even begin to hear my mam's voice, her scepticism weighing me down.

'Isn't it about time you gave up all that ridiculous running stuff, our Julie? Haven't you got anything better to do?'

But my legs carry on along the defined route while my mind goes on confused excursions. A few more hedge-lined tarmac miles are behind me when I pass my favourite garden centre and start thinking about the plants I have bought there. The willow, the amelanchier, the magnolias, the clematis, the jasmine, the rowan, the crab apple, the dogwoods, the roses, the acer, the cherry, and most of all the elder. These plants are all important to me but the elder is my special tree. In folklore the elder has a spirit—the *Elder Mother*. Mothering and nurturing can come from a variety of sources. I get some of both from my plants, and from my fells. Which are not mine but rather I am theirs. Every time there is a new plant in my garden, I have a new carer, a being who, not by their conscious intent as far as I know, but just by their presence, looks after me. A source of food and medicine and story. I don't believe in fairies but I do know the power of plants.

Many of my doctor friends are sceptical. They have been indoctrinated by a version of medicine which has sought to stamp out ancestral knowledge. I count myself a scientist, but I also know that our white-coated culture has done one hell of a job on erasing legitimate traditional wisdom. I take thyme for a sore throat, lemon balm for calming, rosemary when I need to think clearly, and lavender and lime flowers when I need to sleep, which are all *evidence-based* medicines. But most of all it is the presence of the plants I am affected by; they remind me that I am an animal in an ecosystem, dependent on other species. Some of the most beautiful writing on the interdependency of species has been penned by Darwin himself. The man who is now lauded for championing the necessity of competition was as enchanted by the relationships between life forms as by the forms themselves. The last paragraph of Darwin's paradigm-shifting work, *On the Origin of Species*, first published in 1859, reads:

> *'It is interesting to contemplate a tangled bank, clothed with many plants of many kinds, with birds singing on the bushes, with various insects flitting about, and with worms crawling through the damp earth, and to reflect that these elaborately constructed forms, so different from each other, and dependent upon each other in so complex a manner, have all been produced by laws acting around us. These laws, taken in the largest sense, being Growth with reproduction; Inheritance...'*

Inheritance... I have lived with a voice inside me which speaks of nothing but shame when it comes to my inheritance; and yet when I see the worms crawling through the damp earth and smell the witch-hazel in my garden, I get a visceral sense of belonging to this earth. Six hundred million years ago, there was a creature alive which gave rise to both me and the worms. Despite the traumas that tell me that everything about myself is wrong, that I was a mistake, there are other feelings, much deeper, that connect me to the world and weave me into the tangled bank.

Sometimes I begin to wonder about my family tree. There must have been something worthwhile passed on; after all I am here, a marker of the survival of my lineage. Yet I chose not to have children. This was a very considered choice, but still there are moments when I wonder if I am somehow *less* because of it. I don't feel less. Not every woman has to physically give birth as part of her role in the ecosystem. In simple terms there are too many of us anyway. I don't feel I have neglected either myself or my species by not being a mother. And I write books and plant trees. I think that, rather than the future survival of my family line, at all costs, there are other motives which impel my life. But my motives are not things I can personally fully lay claim to—I did not invent myself. Like every other animal on this planet, I have a long and complex biological heritage which I can take neither blame nor credit for; I can only try to create something with it.

One of our near neighbours has recently chain-sawed down an elder on his patch. Woods people would never traditionally cut down elders. I feel sick inside for the elder's loss. I grieve for the tree and wonder at my neighbour's capacity to commit such matricide. Running along the road, lost in thoughts of worms and plants, I hear a vehicle coming behind and get well into the verge, aware of stories of runners injured or killed by passing wing mirrors. But then I realise it is our van coming past and seeing Mandy driving to our next rendezvous point is bitter-sweet. I wish she would stop properly—I want to get in. Nobody would have to know. But this run isn't about anybody else so that's a stupid thought. Without saying much, Mandy slows right down, hands me some water, which I guzzle, then give the bottle back through the van window, and she disappears down the road. I have a job to do and there is no point distracting me. And the last few miles on the road are feeling like work, not pleasure.

I was lucky. After my A-levels, in times when full grants were available to kids like me, I did a degree in biology and genetics, starting in 1982, when genetics as a science was in the midst of its own growth spurt. It had become possible to extract DNA from cells and unravel its code by analysing the sequence of molecules contained within specific genes. I was fascinated and bursting with excitement and understood the possibilities for discovery. Never before had we been able to look into our cells, understand our DNA and begin to understand how we ourselves were put together.

Until the early 1950s nobody knew exactly what DNA was, and now it's common knowledge, part of everyday language. I even heard a football coach on the news the other day saying, 'It could not be any other way—it's in the club's DNA', talking about Manchester United. The metaphor has become universal. DNA—it's what we inherit that we cannot change. Except that DNA has turned from a molecule into a trope. An overused simplification. Perhaps Mr Darwin himself was not as arrogantly certain of his own theory as we assume he was. Of course, in a Christian society he was reticent about publicly denouncing the Book of Genesis. But he also acknowledged he might not have the whole thing sewn up and that Mr Lamarck might have been onto something too. And in the last thirty years the science of biology has progressed at an impressive pace. It has become evident that DNA is not a simple coding machine that determines our fate, as we thought it was when I was an undergraduate.

When I was studying at York, I thought my university teachers were the great keepers of all important knowledge. To say I respected them would be an understatement. Granted some of them had weird hair and very posh accents and some even committed the ultimate sin of wearing socks with their sandals. Although they could not be relied on for sartorial elegance, they were unanimous and clear that elegance had always been an esteemed principle in science. If theories looked messy and complicated, they were probably wrong. Which betrays how science is not just a method of finding objective truth; it is also a value system, as much as any other. A system that values elegance, neatness and beauty, as well as reality and reliability. I don't know of many famous scientists from Sunderland, other than St Bede, the man my school was named after. Maybe this is because Sunderland folk understand that life is messy.

St Bede wrote about the Earth's spherical movements, attempting to explain seasons, moon phases and tides, which was very advanced in the year 725 AD. On his quest to understand the world systematically, Bede was not your average Mackem. Looking for order in the wild world is an antidote to all our human mess and it also opens the possibility of controlling our own destiny. Understanding the laws of nature helps us to manipulate the world to our advantage. At my university, we young scientists were encouraged to think that genetics was clear and elegant. DNA, inheritance, genetic selection—all so beautifully simple. We love to keep things simple, even when they're not.

As students we quickly developed habits and occupied our own niches within our academic and social groups. We would normally sit in the same places in the main lecture theatre. I would be about two-thirds of the way back on the left, from where I had a great view of Shergar, the horse's skeleton, which stood quietly, with grace and presence, in the corner. We all loved Shergar. We named him midway through our first year when the famous racehorse himself was kidnapped and never found. The day we were given a lecture on the evolution of biomechanics, using Shergar as the prop, we spilled out of the hall afterwards, all buzzing and amazed. Sometimes in that lecture theatre and in those labs at York I had an addictive surge of happiness. Learning was biology too; I could almost feel my own neurons branching, growing and making connections.

In my enthusiasm I had started getting up at 6am to go for a run, then I would eat a large bowl of porridge and then do an hour's study before the 9.15 lecture. At lunchtime I would go for another run and, depending on the afternoon schedule, I would sometimes have time for the library. Of all the places I had yet been in my life, I loved York University Library the most. To come through the glass doors, into the arms of all that knowledge, was to transcend all the invisible boundaries that held me back. If my lunchtime run had been hard, I would sometimes find a quiet seat, maybe trespass into physics or even history, and just sit there. The silence, the weighty furniture, the sun shafts picking out dust specks in the air, and hundreds and thousands of precisely catalogued books. This was a sanctified place.

I would pick a book for my lap so as to appear legitimate but often I would snooze or just sit inhaling the books as if the knowledge in their pages would osmose to my brain via my nostrils and lungs. That woody, heavy, bookish smell was pure comfort. I wouldn't choose the book for its contents but its feel. If it felt beautiful, I would sit with it, maybe even open it and run my hands over the pages, as if my fingers were another portal for the knowledge to flow in. I would let my eyes close and surrender to a gorgeous snoozy feeling. I could only ever relax like this if I had also had a good lunchtime run; and I don't know that I had ever felt it before—such calm, such peace, such safety. It was so transporting that for a short while I would forget the chewing anxiety which told me I did not belong here.

'University—where the heck did you get that idea? And after that what will you do? You divunt want to get left on the shelf, du ya?'

I'm sure that my mam's fears would only have been heightened if she could have witnessed my love of the library. Perhaps education was like running. Dangerous.

At York I was two different people at once. I was the student in love with her subject and an impostor from an underclass. In his autobiography Brendan Foster said he considered deliberately changing his accent when he went to Sussex University. But he didn't. When you take northern kids to posh gigs we can often feel out of place. Good for Brendan—he remained himself. I was too convinced I did not belong, too scared, and besides nobody could understand a word I said. I lived in a friendly house with nine other students. We all got on well once they stopped feeling insulted by my phrasing, such as 'ee, why ya bugger' (which in Sunderland was a simple expression of interest in what was being said and not, as my housemates first thought, an accusation of sexual indiscretion). I spent the first term, as my brother would put it, 'larnin how te tark proper'. I was desperate to be accepted into this intelligent elegant world and kept on feeling I simply wasn't made from the right blueprint. Yet the library had the power to melt all that anxiety away. In the library I was just there, wrapped up and safe.

And in the lab, I was shown how to extract DNA from cells; and after many painstaking hours at the bench, a process which would take minutes now, I ended up with a very small white speck in the bottom of a tiny plastic tube. That was DNA. What was it about this stuff that was so special? I was already very familiar with the molecular shape of DNA as shown in textbooks. The classic double helix. As soon as you see the structure of DNA it is easy to see how the molecule can carry a code, and how it can unzip down the middle to make copies of itself to pass on the code. And my teachers were right—there is an elegant simplicity in how it works.

We had a very simple model of how DNA works back in the 1980s. It was beautiful. But forty years later we understand that simple model was not exactly wrong, but it was nowhere near complicated enough to describe what actually happens in real life. It's not often a matter of one gene, one job. For example, there is no single gene for height or intelligence or, as has been said about me, a running gene. Genes are like instruments in an orchestra. If you don't inherit a good piano, then playing certain pieces of Rachmaninov might be tricky; but there's still a lot of other music you can make with the instrument you have. Our bodies are an orchestra of many genes and they interact together to make the music of ourselves. The genes are only the instruments; they give us our potential. But the complexity of the score, the skill and emotion with which the music is played—that is an orchestration between our genes and our world. There are hundreds of genes in my body which gave me my potential to run, and hundreds which limit that potential. Not all of our genes are active all the time, and just like the instruments in the orchestra, my genes listen to each other and respond to each other. We are only beginning to uncover the complexities. Running or football, integrity or kindness—these are not in our genes, any more than Mozart is in a violin.

I have manged to get beyond the mainline railway and the M6 motorway is far behind, but there is one last obstacle ahead of me before the end of day one's run. I'm scared of the prospect of crossing the A66 but have chosen a crossing point where both the drivers and I have a good view of the road. I'm standing on the verge, breathing in fumes, waiting for a gap.

If I were driving along this road myself, as I sometimes do, I would have a different perspective. They may be ugly but we need roads and cars and all that; they are just part of life. But ugliness provokes a heavy feeling inside me, reminding me of the lead weights that were stuck in my legs and my guts when I was young. All this internal strife is passing quickly and semi-consciously, in the space of less than a few seconds, then I see a gap—I'm going for it. Safely across the road, I nip onto the grass verge, then I find a small wooden stile over a fence into a manicured green grazing field. My feet are off the tarmac and it's only three miles to our campsite for tonight. Because of Covid, and wanting to be sure we would get somewhere to park up that was both comfortable and allowed, we have pre-booked a place at Long Marton Campsite. Not long now and I'll be enjoying a shower.

Map in hand, following every little feature, I approach a farm along a well-made track. Not a thing of beauty, the farm is mainly huge modern barns with incarcerated livestock. Such a hypocrite I am. I eat, I use transport, I order things on the internet that arrive in vans. But is it hypocritical to feel sad that we need to rely on the ugliness to survive? My task now is to find where the footpath exits from the agricultural metropolis. It's not obvious. The configuration of buildings on the map doesn't quite seem to correspond to reality. Or is it my overheated thirsty brain not being able to match things up?

I'll try going through this gate—maybe there is a faint hint of a trod around the side of this field. Along the edge of the field, I can manage a trot but my legs are tired. There is no further gate or stile but a small weakness in the barbed-wire fence where others have obviously crossed. I commit a sin against the Countryside Code and clamber over, then head on into a thicket of trees. Can't run now—my legs are getting more and more entangled in briars and thick vegetation. I'm in Darwin's tangled bank. Maybe I should go back and find a better route. No—press on. It'll work out.

I emerge by a little river, very pretty and overhung with willow and alder. Hmm… there's a steep bank down into it and, although the water is cooling, it's deeper and faster flowing than I'd bargained for, and I struggle not to get swept off my feet. Trainers slipping on the slimy shifting river stones, I scrabble up to the opposite bank and pull on some roots to get me up. This isn't funny any more.

I sit down under the trees, desperately trying to make sense of the map which has turned into hieroglyphics. I'm done in. I've run about 35 miles and I'm hot and sore and scratched and lost. What an idiot. I haven't brought a compass because I thought I wouldn't need one on a sunny lowland run. I have my phone but never use it for any sort of navigation and don't even know how to use Google Maps.

I struggle out of the trees and over another fence. Green rolling hills in front but I can see nothing of the hoped-for campsite. Must be over the side of that next small hill. I drag my achy legs upwards and get out my phone. I last saw Mandy over an hour and a half ago in a village before the A66 and expected to be at the day's end within about 45 minutes from there. It is at least a relief to hear her voice.

'Hello—where are you?' Walking up to another fence, I begin climbing over while responding. 'I don't know—arrrgggghhhhhh!! Oh Christ. Shit. Arrhhhggggh! Fucking hell. Oh my God!'

'Jules—what's going on? Are you alright? What's happening?'

'Oh God. I've just been electrocuted by a fence.'

'Are you alright?'

'Oh, I don't know. My arm's killing me. I feel a bit weird and I don't know where I am.'

'I'll try walking back along your route from the campsite and see if I can see you.'

Numerous phone calls later.

'What can you see now?'

'I'm on a bridleway with hawthorn hedges.'

'Yes. I'm on that. Keep going and you'll see me.'

'What direction is the sun in as you are walking?'

'In front.'

'Oh, it's in front of me as well, I'll turn round'.

At last, a smiling woman and waggy-tailed hound come into view and we stroll back to the campsite, where food, stretching and a shower await. I am stiff and sore from the road and the heat. But tomorrow promises to be a very different kind of run. Daunted and excited, as the evening draws in I settle down in the van, serenaded by owls, and try to sleep. Breakfast, food and clothing are all sorted, ready for another early start.

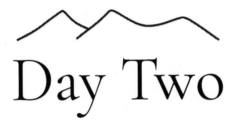

Day Two

Home-walk in Spring

The dog is always eager for a walk before breakfast and her happy
expectation
draws me out.

Beyond the gate, into the meadow, along by the river and it's by then
I start to breathe.

The morning air has lost its bite, shoots poke through,
buds begin.

I am tempted to feel lucky against the canvas of my ever-present guilt
at this good fortune.

Breathe deep now, don't sniff hesitantly from this spectacular atmosphere.
I am here.

I am woven into the fabric of this day. I had mistaken my life for a loose
thread until
someone stitched me in.

6 *The Script*

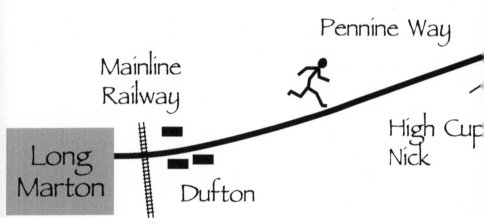

Pennine Way

Mainline
Railway

Long
Marton

Dufton

High Cup
Nick

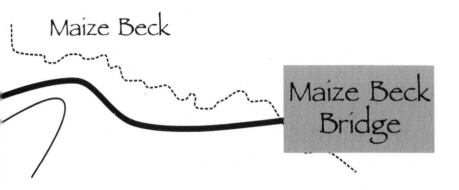

Maize Beck

Maize Beck
Bridge

No mother is ever, completely,
a child's idea of what a mother should be,
and I suppose it works the other way
around as well. But despite everything,
we didn't do too badly by one another…

Margaret Atwood, The Handmaid's Tale

B eing a student in York I never felt confident, but I did feel excited. I was animated by the energy generated by constantly learning, and I was calmed by the feel of the leafy campus and the sense of history embodied in the city's buildings. I loved my new friends and most of all—well, second only to the library—I loved being in the cross-country team. Training hard midweek in a pack of runners, driving each other ever faster, and then seeing my name posted on the notice board when I was picked for a weekend race—I tingled with the scary thrill of it. The races were brutal, muddy and short. But I got quicker with each one; and near the end of the first year I went back to Sunderland for a weekend, to run my first ever road race—the third edition of the Great North Run—in 1983.

The night before the race I was back in my childhood bed feeling an uneasy queasiness. I couldn't tell if this was nerves about the next day or fears of the past. Early the next morning I got the number twenty-three bus into town from the end of our road and then a train to Newcastle. Mam and Tom would be coming to South Shields on the coast to see me finish the race and pick me up. I only have one memory of the Great North Run and, even then, it's not from during the event but watching it on telly afterwards. Strange that I ran the race and I cannot tell you anything about it. I don't remember the start line, the finish line or anything in between; and no matter how much I delve into my memory banks, the race itself is simply a blank. But I remember, clear as day, what happened afterwards.

As I neared the end of the race, Mam and Tom hadn't spotted me, so they had stood on the corner before the finish line, waiting a long time for me to come past. Not finding them anywhere amongst the crowds, I used the sunny afternoon to best advantage and walked down the coast to Marsden beach with its impressive 100-foot-tall sea-stack and nice bar. It's really quite exotic. After two pints of Guinness, I got the bus home to Sunderland and let myself in to Mam's house with my Yale key on its Sunderland Football Club keyring. I lay on the brown velvety sofa in our small front room, with the swirly patterned carpet and the purple and fawn coloured flock wallpaper which Mam had skilfully hung without a single pattern mismatch at the joins. I switched on the telly, amazed to be seeing a report of the race. The race I had just taken part in. Then the front door burst open and I could tell by the pitch of her voice she'd blown a fuse.

'Where *were* you? We waited ages. We never saw you. Worra a waste of time. Wu'll not be doing that again, will wu Tom?'

'Well, it wasn't really Julie's fault, pet.'

At least Tom stood up for me a bit, but Mam was having none of it.

'Why weren't you taking notice? You should've seen us. And I can't believe yu'v been drinking Guinness, that's a disgrace. I bet it costs a fortune at Marsden Grotto. Sometimes I just wish yu'd act like a normal daughter! I just give up with you, our Julie. I'll put the kettle on.'

It was an inglorious start to my road running career. She did have a point about the Guinness. Although some studies have shown beer to be a highly effective recovery drink after a long run, there's a fair bit of alcohol in two pints for an eight-stone weakling. Mind you, drinking was something I had definitely had good training in—and putting away my own blood volume in ale was no problem to me. After all, I'm pretty sure that I am my father's daughter.

After the tea, and homemade rock buns, Mam's culinary speciality, I packed up my stuff to get the train back to York, wishing in my heart I would never have to come back to Sunderland but knowing I would. Whether I liked it or not, Mam had a hold over me. I thought she had—locked away in some seldom-visited place—the love and safety I was searching for and the approval I needed. I don't really know if I enjoyed the Great North Run because all I remember is the disappointment of her reaction. And I had been away for months, so it felt horrible, to be back in our house, which had been a school of violence, where I had learned what women were really for. My guts churned every time I came down Tilbury Road, where we had lived at number 162 since I had been a babe in arms. I felt sick but I still came, desperately drawn. It was time I broke free of that feeling. I needed to put this place behind me. This Sunderland me was not me. I went back to York, determined to be somebody else.

There's no moon and the lanes leading out of the campsite are resting in a thick black quiet. I'm living in the world created by the beam of my head torch. I have left Mandy and Moss in our cosy van and begun easing my body into a gentle run. After about twenty minutes, daylight slides its way over the English Pennines, extending its reach towards me. Having trotted along some hawthorn-guarded lanes, I come into the village of Dufton and switch off my light. I am looking at the sleepy sandstone cottages and trying to remember something about the summer before my first year at university, when I walked the Pennine Way with my boyfriend David. We must have passed this way.

David was a Tyneside lad so we were another inter-tribal Geordie-Mackem match. We had met at a youth hostel while I was out cycling. It was a good summer. We camped every night of the 268-mile-long walk in a tiny tent, my new prize possession; and the greatest treat was finding a pub and having a pint at the end of the day. Stag Inn at Dufton, a small cottage-like pub melding into the middle of the terrace—there it is—still just as I remember. I slow right down to look again and take it in. In my mind's eye I see us, two teenagers in shorts and muddy boots with suntanned legs and rosy faces, and two pints of Tetley's beer and a packet of crisps on the table.

Despite the whole world of science trying to find something which can be called *objectivity*, it's impossible ever to just look at anything and only see the information the light is relaying to the back of the eye. There is always the context and interpretation of memory tied up with every sight and sound and smell. You don't even need a nervous system to have a memory. According to theories of quantum entanglement, even subatomic particles have memory. The laws of nature forbid anything ever to be truly forgotten.

Understanding that nobody else can see through my eyes, I suddenly feel very empty and lonely. I wonder what happened to my sixth-form friend Linda, to David, to my colleagues in my biology class and even to Mrs Colclough. I feel guilty and ashamed of myself for not keeping in touch. At the time I just needed to move on, but now I feel terrible. Did I abandon them? A mixture of nostalgia, grief and guilt pulses around within me as I trot quietly on, wondering how much I have carelessly lost.

The village is almost silent. The dawn has been grey and cloudy. I'm paying close attention to the map and looking for the lane that will lead me to the Pennine Way. I feel displaced. A man out walking his dog passes on the other side of the road looking at me blankly with no acknowledgment. Maybe I shouldn't be here? It feels like I am doing something wrong but I don't understand what rule I'm transgressing against. My sense of un-entitlement is profound.

I see the bridleway sign and turn left onto the rough lane leading to the moor. My legs are feeling a bit heavy and I struggle to keep running as the gradient steepens. Breaking into a fast walk, I try and urge myself on. I'm disappointed about the sensations of pain in my back and pelvis and I feel a million years old. I have rose-tinted memories of the runner I once was. All I can see is a long winding lane extending into the far distance up to the cloud-covered moor. My inner judge runs with me every step of my weary way. The monkey on my back whose job it is to tell me how I've failed, how I'm not good enough, and never will be. I know it's all rubbish. Good enough for what and by whose standards?

I don't hold with notions of success and failure and status. I rail against those conservative social constructs and I know, in my thinking mind, that my insecurities are all a product of conditioning and the voices of my past coming to taunt me. But my body doesn't know, my body still feels wrong. I start wondering, as I settle into a manageable pace up the hill, if you take the intellectual interpretation out of it, how my body is telling my story. What is my sacral bone saying about the way it was smashed to pieces and how it has rebuilt itself? What is my spine saying about how it came to be that funny painful shape? What are my muscles saying about how they are always tense and ready to run when threats appear? I am an animal. I started from a sperm and an egg. I did not seek my own manufacture. I am biology built on billions of years of experience. There must be a place for me in the ecosystem. I'm alive.

I realise I have broken into running again, up the stone-strewn track onto the moor. I'm running. I'm running and I'm tearful, without being able to understand why. A kind of knifeless neurosurgery seems to be taking place. I stand still for a moment on the grey hillside and shout into the mist at the top of my voice, without addressing anyone in particular, 'Fuck off!'

I've no idea why I felt the need to do that; I just want the tension inside to release, and I carry on running as the gradient lessens.

The route leads up along the edge of High Cup Nick, the huge and perfectly U-shaped glacial valley known as England's Grand Canyon, which cuts through a band of dolerite rock, the Whin Sill, that runs all the way across to the North Sea. Being keener on the excitement of mountains and crags than the melancholy of moors, I usually neglect the Pennines. Walking the Pennine Way forty years ago was my last visit to High Cup Nick and I've been looking forward to seeing it again. But coming to such a place is not just a matter of seeing. Being in a landscape affects me, moves my being in different ways, and there is something about moorland which challenges me. The open expanses of undulating ground feel empty; and like a laughter-less empty house, that emptiness can become an emotion of lack which reaches into the unfilled gaps within me. The moors are beautiful and less disturbed by hordes of humans than the bigger hills but maybe there is a reason I neglect them. Open moors insist on an emotion of openness within me, an honesty about how I really feel. Much easier to be in mountains, which tap into stamina, bravery and my sense of adventure.

I am running along the rim of the valley. The edge is just to my right; from there it plunges spectacularly over steep scree into the glacier-gouged scoop. Then everything disappears completely into a grey fog. I thought the Pennine Way would be easy to follow. But the big track has turned into a choice of thin trods through fading heather. I begin to wonder if I have followed the edge of the Nick all the way along and am now going back on myself on the other side. I stop to get out the compass and try to figure out where I am. But I've been running without keeping track of how far I've come, and I'm enveloped in cloud which wets my hair. Because of my distracting emotions and the three-metre visibility, my sense of direction is sketchy.

There is a kind of comfort in being lost. The challenge of finding myself focuses my practical mind. I am lost on a lonely clagged-in moor and something about the gloom is soothing. The greyness offers an empathy which allows me not to fear my sadness. To allow myself to be sad sometimes is a great gift and even a necessity. In Darwin's time, sadness was prized; melancholy was a respectable and refined emotion. All I am finding on the moor is seemingly random tall wooden posts which display coloured squares and triangles. Something to do with the grouse and pheasant shooting no doubt, but no help for finding my route. It occurs to me that shooting season has just started, but thankfully there's no sign or sound of gratuitously violent men with guns taking pleasure in an avian massacre. Traditional countryside sport, they call it.

Under the heather the black peat is breathing. Here and there, huge oozing wounds of open peat gape across the ruptured skin of the moor. It's not a healthy place this; it's a wounded excoriation of the woodland and upland scrub that has been annihilated from the English uplands. In the silent cloudy morning, I run round in circles in the scratchy heather until I figure it out, and then begin running down the side of the stream draining the watershed eastwards. This must be right. But it seems a very small path for the Pennine Way. I am not certain, but I run on, and different trods seem to be converging into a more defined path. Yes, this must be my route. The stream is a friend showing me the way; the sound of running water begins to dispel the tension of silence.

Always keen not to have anything to do with the girl I grew out of—I became somebody else. I went through many iterations of somebody else. I was a genetics researcher; I was a science teacher; I was an outdoor education teacher; I was a medical student; and for a long time, I was a doctor. I have spent most of my adulthood working in medicine and it was work I was motivated to do. In childlike fashion I believed in its innate goodness, and thought that, by association, practising medicine might also make me good. But I was hopeless at getting on with most of my colleagues in general practice. While I was concerned with how and why people suffered and what could be done to ease their pain, my fellow doctors seemed mostly concerned with evidence, targets, pathways, practice income and retirement funds.

There are wonderful doctors in the world, and I did come across some. But most I worked with seemed tragically brainwashed by algorithms. This I found depressing. And it was another source of my sense of being a weirdo. I questioned many guidelines. I was sometimes labelled a maverick and I was an easy target for bullying; a laughable idealist. Where I was at home was on the inside of a consultation, listening to a person's story. Reading a person's body through my ears and eyes and stethoscope and hands. In modern medicine it is rare to have an ongoing relationship with the same patient or family. I developed the art of quickly building trust and connection. I tried to make a single encounter count and reverberate long after it was over.

I was once on a bike ride through an out-of-the-way village in Yorkshire; covered in muck and sweat, I had a pitstop at a post office which was advertising coffee and homemade flapjacks. A woman popped her head round the side of the shelves of crisps and fizzy cans.

'It's *You!*'

'Hello.'

'I never thought I'd see you again. You saved my life. You were the only one who listened to me.'

I knew who she was. I had been berated by my consultant, at the time she'd been in hospital, for spending time on what he called 'counselling' when I was meant to be learning obstetrics. Although the coffee and flapjacks were welcome, that woman's words and smile were the kind of nourishment that really kept me going.

But through all my iterations of somebody, I did always go back to Sunderland to see my mam. I would regularly feel the familiar sickness as I drove down our street. I would regularly worry about her after Tom died and she grew old. I would survey the cupboards to see what she had in, and what she'd been eating. We would go to the supermarket and stock up.

'Here's some of that muesli you said you liked when you came to our house, Mam.'

She would look sheepish, then I'd find it replaced with a cheap box of Cornflakes.

'Mam, you can have the Cornflakes as well as the muesli. Where's those nuts I put in? I thought you liked them?'

'No. Too dear, pet. I don't need much. It's only me.'

'It doesn't matter, Mam. And anyway, I'm paying. You can have some fresh orange, not just the squash; that's full of additives.'

'I just want what I'm used to, pet, let's not argue. Ee, me back's killing me anyway. I'll have to sit down.'

We'd get home and I would put the shopping away and help her eat the cheap biscuits over a pot of tea made with one-pence teabags. How stupid was I, suggesting we get the English Breakfast? As Mam observed, it costs more than double.

'You've never had a clue about housekeeping and learning how to manage, have yu?'

And when it came time to leave her, I was desperate to get out the door and heartbroken to go at the same time. I would need to have the music cassettes ready in the car. How would I have survived those nights over the A66 if it hadn't been for Annie Lennox, Kate Bush,

Leonard Cohen and Dire Straits? Mark Knopfler, another son of Tyneside, had a voice which was tender and yet defiant. Like his Romeo I wanted to know love that would shine like the stars and last until I die, and that there was a place for me. And with the volume turned to the max I would cry till I had hardly any salt or water left to cry with. I would torture myself with the idea that she knew about, or suspected, what had happened to me in the caravan. Or she didn't know. Or she knew but didn't believe it. And was that the same as not knowing? And either way, those journeys from her house back to my own home in Cumbria, where I'd settled, were a burning kind of hell. I hated her, I hated my family, I wanted nothing to do with her and I wanted her love like nothing else on Earth. I was furious with my own pain. The past is the past—just forget it. But it wouldn't take much to drive off the road at over seventy. It probably wouldn't even hurt much, and then all this torture would be over. Dazzled by oncoming headlights and trying to keep a grip on the wheel, I thought maybe there was something else I could do. I could slip her something, make it look like a natural death. Sometimes it felt like it was her or me. Jesus Christ, what kind of a bastard was I to think of killing my own mother? You can't get any lower than that in life, surely.

But later, when I neared my own home, I knew there was always something else I could do—I could go for a run. I'd go in the night when I got back from Sunderland, through little lanes and over familiar fields, with a head torch and with the owls. Normally running puts your heart rate up, but these runs put mine back down again. Then after the run I could get into bed with Mandy. And sleep.

Up on the moor the clouds are breathing out water which condenses on my warm body, beading on my running shirt, then everything starts to change. The grey is getting lighter. The air is becoming almost white, and I sense there is something behind the white. Blue. Blue starts coming. Now the whole air is blue and yellow with sunshine. And I hear the larks. Maybe the larks were singing before, they do it even when it's raining, but my ears open up to them much more when the sun comes out.

Sunshine doesn't always stop me feeling sad. Sometimes sunshine provokes me to feel sad. When it's sunny and I'm stuck inside; or I'm somewhere ugly, like the car park of a motorway service station or walking into a claustrophobic airless hospital ward. Some places feel like an insult to sunshine, a waste of it. It's much easier to be in places like that when it's raining. It's okay to feel sad when my body can shiver with damp and feel the tears of clouds. There's empathy in that. But sunshine in the wrong context is terribly insensitive.

I am definitely back on the right route now but still surprised at how small the Pennine Way is at this stage. The heather gives way to tussocky nibbed grass. The nibblers, the upland Swaledale sheep with black faces and curly wool, are unperturbed by my presence and nibble on. I come to a footbridge, half broken down, but a definite landmark and something to form a firm link between the world and the map. The bridge is oddly urban-looking, with a steel framework for a base, and broken lattices of wood on top, making it look like a piece of Meccano.

I lie down in the sunshine on the sheep-mown grass and listen to the larks and the travelling stream. Rummaging in my rucksack, I pull out a cheese sandwich. In no rush now, I stretch out my back and warm through. In different circumstances I could have let myself doze off.

I was with Mam, sitting at the front window table in her favorite café, The Bungalow, overlooking Seaburn Harbour in Sunderland. Mam couldn't walk far when she was in her eighties but she enjoyed the view of the harbour and the smell of the sea air. I would dutifully take her there on my visits. Helping her in and out of my red Nissan Micra, taking her bony arm and steadying her balance. The feel of her was precarious and fleshless by now. Her appetite was dwindling. She would never get through a plate of food in the café but would always ask for extra napkins to take home what she couldn't manage. It's stupid to pay for food and then let it go to waste. That day our luck was in, and we got the window seats with a bird's eye view of the harbour's curvaceous piers and the shining sea. Occasionally a huge container ship would appear on the horizon and little sailing dinghies would furl across the water near the shore. We could watch the sea forever.

There would always be some embarrassment at the Bungalow Café. I was in my forties, having made a career in medicine, but I might as well have been a teenager as far as Mam was concerned. And something far too personal and inappropriate would be said to the waitress or fellow lunchers.

'Ee, me daughter's come to visit from the Lake District. She's got a nice house over there. No bairns though. She lives with another woman. Some people think it's bad but I cannut see owt wrong with it. What d'you think?'

I'd steel myself and smile; after all, I'd had decades of practice at weathering such humiliations. But once we were settled and the generous teapot arrived, Mam got down to the business of telling me a story. I didn't need to pay attention, I had heard them all several hundred times. I could just nod every now and then, fill her cup at intervals, and enjoy the view. She was saying something about when Aunty Dinah last came from Australia. How Dinah (my mother's aunty and my great-aunty) had been to Gateshead

Stadium to unveil a plaque in honor of her father, Jack Nowell. Hang on. Was this a new story? I thought she might have been making it up. I started asking questions about this mysterious character Jack Nowell.

'Yes, yu know.' Mam always said that when I didn't have a clue. 'Jack Nowell.'

'Was he your grandfather?'

'Yes, he was me grandar, Aunty Dinah's dad. You know, he was the founder of Gateshead Harriers.'

'What? My great-grandfather was the founder of Gateshead Harriers!'

'Yes, yu know! Aunty Dinah met Brendan Foster. She went to the Tartan Track.'

Why had she never told me this? Had she told me but I hadn't been listening? Was she making it up or had she got confused? Why had I loved running all these years? I loved it as a kid on the beach. I loved it at university. For a while I was too busy working to run much, but then I loved it again when I moved to Cumbria and, in my forties, I began running on the fells and finding freedom and flow on hills. I'd run road races, cross-country races, fell races, ultra-marathons and mountain marathons. I'd run Brendan Foster's Great North Run and worn the T-shirt with its logo of the Tyne Bridge. Brendan himself was a Gateshead Harrier. All this time I had felt like an impostor in a world I ought not to belong to. I ought to be a mother in Sunderland. Who did I think I was—being a medical doctor and winning races?

I had tried to feel respectable for a long time, but all the shame I ever felt was carried inside my body. I'd always known I was guilty, right from the start, even if I was never clear about what I was guilty of. I understand that kids often feel responsible for crimes they did not commit. But intellectual understanding does not take away what the body holds onto. Guilt and shame were the food I ate and the air I breathed; they became part of my physical make-up. And running somehow helped to detoxify me. It was exciting to run in races and run with friends and have goals and ambitions but really my running has always been a way of my body letting go. It's not something I can think about. It's purely of the body, involving muscles and nerves and heartbeats and breath. Running was my medicine but it only worked in regular doses. I often felt the only thing that would really ease the strain of pretending would be to give in and play the part I was destined for in the first place. To drink like my dad, to resign like my mother.

But what if the story I'd come to believe about my own destiny was all wrong in the first place?

I am the great-granddaughter of the founder of the famous Gateshead Harriers. I stared out to sea. Incredulous. Somebody had just swapped my script.

The Nowell Family Tree

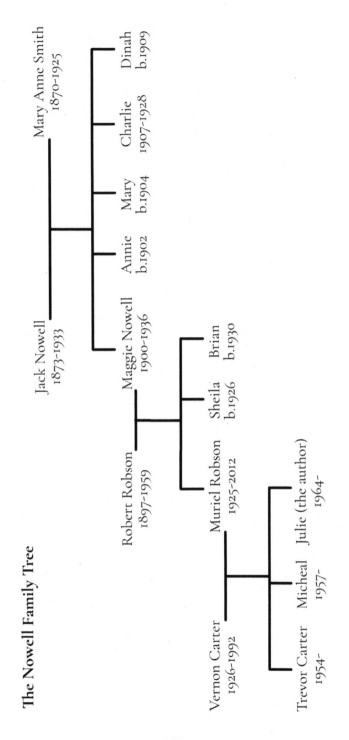

Roses

I am a woman from your womb
      an unconsented conception
            unimagined.

Born naked and wanting
      warmth, breastmilk
            a future.

Unwashed but not unclean
      unprotected, unencouraged,
            unsmothered.

Unmothered but not unloved
      unrecognised but not
            unwanted.

Undaunted I will tint my lens
      with roses for you
         holding hands,
            on your death bed
            understood.

7 *Blood of Her Blood*

Cow Green Reservoir

Maize Beck
Bridge

Cauldron
Snout

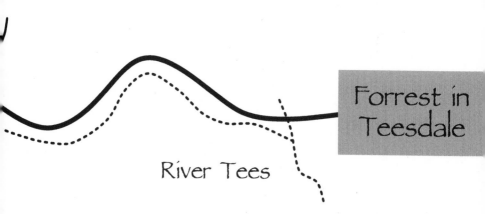

Forrest in Teesdale

River Tees

Hearing voices is not a sign of illness—
it's a sign of our ability to survive.

Rachel Waddingham, Intervoiceonline.org

I t was late on a Sunday night in June, and from my consulting
room in Accident and Emergency in Whitehaven on Cumbria's
west coast I was on the phone to a doctor on the medical admissions
ward of Sunderland Hospital. It wasn't long after the conversation
at the Bungalow Café. I put the phone down and carried on
working. There was a waiting room full of patients. It took three
more consultations before I came to my senses. Then, on my way
back down from the children's ward, after escorting an asthmatic
little boy sucking oxygen from a bottle bigger than himself and
clinging to his bewildered mum's hand, I told my colleague about
the phone call from Sunderland.

'Go!' she insisted. 'Go now!'

'I don't want to just leave you with all this lot.'

The waiting area was crammed but my colleague was calm and
supportive.

'You have to leave now Julie. These people are not your mother!'

I logged off, grabbed my bag and got home at midnight. Luckily
our neighbor was a night owl and loved Moss. Our unfortunate
hound was due at the vet's at 7.30 the next morning to be spayed.
Sometimes small acts of kindness go a long way and we really
appreciated the help.

'No problem. I'll take her to the vet's and pick her up and nurse
her until you get back. Just don't worry about it. Anything else I
can do?'

We left our sleepy dog in good hands and Mandy drove through the darkness on quiet easy roads. I was in a trance as we headed east on the familiar route, towards the midsummer dawn. At 4am it was getting light as I stumbled through the steel and glass doors of the hospital and stood in front of an array of signposts to the wards... and could not read a word. They were just white shapes on blue, green and red backgrounds. I had no way of making any sense of either the scrambled letters on the wall or the pixelated emotions running through my body. Panic flooded in, as I was desperate to find Mam.

Oh Christ, I hoped she wasn't dead. Even on good days hospitals have a way of making me feel inadequate and terrified. I've spent years of my life inside hospitals, trying to be a reassuring and competent grown-up, yet they always make me feel a bit sick. Stupid choice for a job then—being a doctor? And there I was, rooted to the spot in front of the signposts, unable to read or speak.

'It's down that way. Medical Assessment Unit.'

Mandy's voice pulled me back to reality as she pointed the way, and soon we were there, at Mam's bedside. I held her ice-cold hand. She opened her eyes and smiled and began to chat.

'Are you alright pet? Mandy's here as well, that's nice. How's the dog, pet? Have yu brought it with yu? Is it raining outside pet?'

I used to find it infuriating—how she could ignore a herd of elephants charging through any room to concentrate on small talk of no consequence. But in that moment, I understood what all the small talk had been saying. We had driven each other mad all these years. Her being her, and me being me, and each wishing the other could be a bit more like our ideal model of what a mother or a daughter should be. But that morning I felt as if every cell in my body must have its own tiny heart and all those hearts were breaking at once. I had hated Mam's brashness, her ability to twist the truth, her indiscretions and prejudices. But I was *made* of her. Blood of her blood. Holding her cold hand, I felt her shivering, and she couldn't understand, when I said it was a lovely sunny morning, why she was freezing.

'It cannut be. I'm perished pet. Can yu ask the nurse for another blanket? Anyway, what are yu gunna do now pet?'

As if she half-expected me to be eager to leave, to have more pressing things on my agenda.

'I am going to stay here with you, Mam.'

'Oh, that's nice, pet.'

'I love you, Mam.'

'I love you, pet.'

She closed her eyes, kept hold of my hand, and dozed off. As the drip-drip-drip of crystal-clear fluid running through a tube into her arm measured out the moments, I sat there holding her cold hand, thinking about how she'd held my hand in the sea, thinking about how, through all these years, somehow, we'd both stayed afloat.

Lying in the sunshine beside Maize Beck, it dawns on me that I have crossed the watershed. From now on I am east of the main Pennine backbone. A check of the map again before rousing myself into action; now I'll be following this stream down into a place called Birkdale. I pull myself up and start walking, then running; as my pace gets faster both the stream and the path get bigger. Everything is sunshine and warmth and quiet; the beck is my only companion. I've seen no one since Dufton and if another human were to appear now it would come as a shock.

After crossing a tributary, I reach a wide four-wheel-drive track and enter a *danger area* of MOD land. There is no live firing but I've read that there is still old ordnance about and it's best to make sure I keep to the track and don't try and sneak in any short cuts. I can still feel an ache in my arm from yesterday's electric shock. Surely electric fences aren't meant to be that powerful. The juxtaposition of sunshine and open moor with a track that is so substantial it feels almost urban is a bit jarring. But it's easy going and there's no chance of getting lost now as I trot on, eager to reach Cauldron Snout, another exciting place I haven't been to since our Pennine Way walk.

I remembered Alfred Wainwright queerly describing it as a 'fine mountain cataract', in his little blue and white book, the *Pennine Way Companion*, which was our text for that pilgrimage. I hadn't understood AW's remark but when I realised that Cauldron Snout waterfall was directly underneath the dam wall of Cow Green Reservoir I wondered if he was being disparaging, as the waterfall might have been a result of the dam; and knowing Wainwright, he probably didn't approve of such an edifice. But AW wrote his pictorial guide in 1966, just before Cow Green was constructed. It is only now—now that I am properly interested in words, and no longer see using a dictionary as a failure—that I see the word 'cataract' does mean a disease of the eye but also has a second meaning of 'waterfall, waterspout, downpour or flood' and that one can also be subjected to a 'cataract of information'.

It is a beautiful thing to read AW's little blue guide again, the very same copy we carried that summer, with pencilled notes in the back about how much we'd spent each day. To read about the 'dark and dimpled' slabs of limestone in the little gorge of Maize Beck and how the path eastwards is 'spangled with thyme, mossy saxifrage, heath bedstraw and tormentil'. There aren't many flowers now in mid-September, the occasional little yellow smile of tormentil and small patch of faded thyme amongst the sedgy grass. I'm not much of a botanist but I am a flower lover. The delicacy of these upland species woven together in a subtle tapestry is only revealed when you look really closely. Their tiny perfection moves me more than a showy garden bloom.

The beck is big enough to deserve the title of river now as the bank steepens off down to my right. I pass some little huts, probably something to do with shooting. The padlocks make me curious as to what's inside. Soon after Birkdale Farm, described by AW as the 'loneliest inhabited place in Westmorland', I can hear the roar of a waterfall. Cauldron Snout is around the corner.

A nurse appeared at Mam's bedside, along with the kind and bleary-eyed medical registrar I had spoken to earlier on the phone. There seemed nothing to discuss, she gave a sympathetic smile and said the consultant would be coming in shortly. He arrived in a flurry of importance at about 6am and pulled us into his office, explaining that he would get Mam down to operating theatre pronto, to try to stop the bleeding in her stomach.

My heart was pounding so hard I could hardly find the breath to speak. I felt faint, as if the walls of the room were closing in, pressing on my chest. I know we are mainly made from water, but until that moment I'd felt like a solid thing. I am just bags of different fluids separated by membranes. Synovial fluid, cerebro-spinal fluid, lymph, urine, interstitial fluid, saliva, stomach acid, mucus, blood, tears. I was just a bag of fluid, dissolving into nothing, in the panic of not being seen by this, this—self-import-ant... fucker. My anger was useful. My anger pulled me back into action.

'I don't want her to die on an operating table with a tube down her throat, surrounded by strangers. Don't take her to theatre. She's dying. Can't you just let us have a few more moments? I won't have her die like that. Please.'

'It's not really up to you though. There's a small chance I could stop the bleeding and I have to do that, if there is any chance at all.'

Mam was by now unconscious and could not choose for herself so the man in the suit was charged with deciding what was *in her best interests*. A minute later an impassive porter arrived with a trolley to wheel Mam away, like he was collecting airport luggage. Suddenly bright red blood covered the blankets and sheets and dripped from the edge of Mam's bed, congealing on the floor.

'She's not going anywhere,' muttered the porter observantly, and quickly disappeared.

Mandy and I whipped the curtains round the bed; and we grabbed every blanket and towel we could, to cover it all up in case Mam opened her eyes and got frightened. Then I was glad I was a doctor, it helped me to be calm and know what to do. I'd dealt with bloodbaths like this before. Quickly covered up and wiped down, Mam was settled, unresponsive; and Mandy went to ask the nurse to prepare an injectable sedative to have on hand, for kindness' sake, just in case Mam did come round. I held Mam's hand. I did not want her to be frightened. And I sat there holding on, and knowing there would be no more small talk, no more evasions, no more stories.

It is a mysterious miracle that in some strange way we had managed to love each other from the start to the end and, despite everything, I cried good tears. For once I was very glad that I had come back to Sunderland. And then I started to be grateful for all the other painful coming backs too.

I sat in the car in the hospital car park in the sunshine and rang my brother. It was the same car park as the one we had arrived in four hours earlier. How can that be? How can the world just passively stay the same when somebody's mother has just died?

Then a day of frenzied bureaucracy unfolded. Undertaker, registrar, council housing office, building society, post office. I got through them all by the end of the day and by next morning I was a patient in yet another hospital, where I was scheduled for ankle surgery. After almost sixty hours of zero sleep the anaesthetic was a godsend. I used to be a great sleeper. When I was a junior doctor (aka NHS slave) I had mastered the art of getting naps in the most awkward places; given the chance of a night in bed, I would be out like a light. Since Mam died, my sleep has rarely been good.

Approaching Cauldron Snout, I feel a bit disappointed that the dam wall is more imposing than the waterfall itself. The grey concrete slope of the Cow Green Reservoir outflow, with a thin veil of water streaming down it, is a miserable feature. At the time of its construction, which was deemed necessary to maintain a reliable water supply to Teesside industry, conservationists protested against the threat to flowers. 'Flowers or jobs' is how politicians tend to frame these things, but if you happen to be a Teesdale violet then the reservoir wiped out ten per cent of your total habitat. Violets don't get to vote but they do have the amazing feature of being cleistogamous. This means the violet flowers that don't open are able to fertilise themselves—as a back-up, in case the open flowers haven't been pollinated. A mixture of genes is better for offspring but, if you can't have that because the plant has become rare and may not have another one near it, then genes from one parent are better than no genes at all.

As I make my way under the dam wall, my mind is wandering and so I forget to check where I'm meant to be headed. I assumed the path was above the steep cliffs of Falcon Clints towering above the north bank of the river, which is now the Tees. Then I look down and see a defined path below me on the narrow floodplain, squeezed between the river and the foot of the crag. To get down to where I should be, I need to descend through thigh-high, leg-grabbing heather on a very steep slope. What an idiot. I'm meant to be good at mountain navigation but now I'm faceplanting and scraping myself down a dangerous slope because I can't follow an obvious route.

At least, in compensation, I get a proper view of the Snout. The churning white-water powering through the rocky ravine is now full of energy—a contrast to the wide weak flow over the dam wall. I reach the bottom of the heather bank and don't really mind that the running along the riverside is becoming rocky and awkward. The place is so spectacular—I can hardly believe it. I begin to think I have underestimated the charms of the north-eastern countryside. A bit further on, I'm running on a wooden boardwalk over a beautiful bog. I'm officially in Teesdale now and no one else is here. It would be nice to spend more time here. I must come back and look for the Teesdale violet, a scarce organism doing its best to survive.

Mam wasn't a regular churchgoer but she was one of those people who loosely adopt Christianity because it's kind of normal and vaguely comforting. Don't worry. Even though life is confusing, somebody up there has a plan. And as long as we say sorry for being innately bad then we'll all be fine, for eternity. Muriel went along with the story and we reckoned she would definitely have wanted a Christian funeral, so we arranged for the vicar to come round to her house, while we were in the middle of clearing it out. My brother and Mandy and I had to work hard, as we only had two weeks' grace from the Council. After that we would have to hand back the keys and would be charged if there was anything left. I wasn't used to entertaining vicars but Mandy, being from a respectable family, was familiar with the protocols; before dashing out on another tip run, she had given firm instructions.

'I've bought a cake. Here. When the vicar comes, make a pot of tea and offer her cake.'

I wasn't that impressed with this deal.

'I'm not getting the cake out for the vicar unless she looks in need of it. If she's the size of the Vicar of Dibley then she's not getting cake.'

Being *upset* might have been a reason for the surfacing of my horrible prejudices about both religion and body mass index but it wasn't an excuse. Mandy arrived back to find my brother and me drinking tea with the very large vicar, and the cake still in the kitchen.

'Hello Vicar, I'm Julie's partner, would you like some cake?'

Mandy does the right thing, unless she feels there's a considered reason to break with protocol. She seems to be able to decide when to follow rules and when to break them. I've always admired that self-confidence. She made a show of offering the cake, just to make me smirk.

I couldn't tell the vicar much about my mother, just the facts really. I couldn't begin to tell her about *her*. What could I have said? Muriel was a kind of accidental anarchist. She never seemed to do the right thing socially. Was it her upbringing or just that she genuinely wasn't that bothered about offending people? Maybe it was neither. She wanted to be liked and accepted and wanted to impress but didn't have any subtlety about that, because the want was so strong. She was child-like in her need to be liked, as if every person she met was a potential source of something she was looking for. Can *you* like me, can *you* admire me, can *you* give me attention, can *you* give me love? Perhaps all her demanding me-me-me-ness was just desperate unmet need. It was only much later that it occurred to me she was anxious, afraid even. She was full of bravado in public and had a justification for everything. What if it had all been fear? Ineptly seeking approval; living in fear of being swallowed up by disapproval, like walking over quicksand.

As I ate the cake and listened to my brother instructing the vicar, something strange happened. I heard Muriel's voice calling from the kitchen, plain as anything. Not in my imagination but in my ears, coming from the kitchen, calling my name.

'Julie. Are you there, pet? Julie.'

I nipped through to the kitchen to check but nobody was there. The vicar was on her second piece of cake when I returned. I'm sceptical of religion and especially of someone who dresses up in a kind of uniform to signify they have a hotline to God. What kind of arrogance is that? To think you have any answers when all the wisdom is only ever found in the questions? But I was to get my comeuppance on the day of the funeral. And still the voice went on.

'Julie. Are you there, pet? Julie. Julie.'

I listened to Mam's hallucinated voice in her kitchen and was surprised the vicar didn't hear it. Her voice came again later that evening while I was using her iron for our funeral shirts. It was real. The air vibrated in my ears; I could feel it.

'Yes Mam. What do you want? Are you alright?'

Then the room was silent and empty. I looked all round, scanning the edges of the ceiling, wondering how she had managed this conjuring trick. Perhaps the vicar knew about such things; but I never asked.

Still on the north bank of the Tees, the cliffs to my left subside but another escarpment called Cronkley Scar rises up on the other side of the water, maintaining my feeling that the river is not meandering but is on a defined and purposeful journey. When the crags peter out entirely the countryside flattens, as I pass the white Widdy Bank farmhouse and try to decide which path will take me directly to the hamlet of Forrest-in-Teesdale and my next rendezvous. The river is taking a break from drama and wending away from me, gently south-eastwards, in readiness for its next big performance at High Force waterfall a few miles downstream. Stiles over drystone walls guide me on thin paths over rough pasture. There are still no humans and no stock in the fields either. I'm glad to notice a buzzard gliding high above. It makes me feel more connected to life to see another animal.

Although I started in Cumbria at sunrise and feel like I've travelled a long way into County Durham, over what AW describes as a 'famous watershed crossing', it's not yet midday. After a while there's no path and I battle on through reedy soft ground, hoping I'll find a footbridge, which I eventually do, but— after some messing about finding gates and trying to avoid climbing fences—I emerge on the road a little to the north of where I intended. Oh well, another couple of miles on the road won't kill me, but it's getting hot again, just like yesterday, and now I'm really looking forward to a cup of tea.

On funeral day the weather didn't hold back. It was bucketing with rain, not drops of rain but great deluging sheets of it, as Mam arrived in her coffin at the Saltwell Park Crematorium in Gateshead. The park she'd played in when she was little, and the park where Jack Nowell had organised hundreds of sports events. Even though Muriel was dead, she managed to make the whole thing very *her*. My brother and I stood outside and greeted the guests. Not a bad turnout. Friends from Muriel's past and distant family connections. A rainbow-coloured wreath of flowers sat on her coffin.

'Where's the vicar?'

The funeral director, my brother and I gazed out into the Gateshead monsoon, hoping God's representative would put in an appearance. Time ticked on. Everyone had been waiting inside for ages. But there was no vicar.

At first, folk had been solemn and quiet but after a bit they got bored and started chatting and telling stories about Muriel across the pews. One mellifluous Mackem I didn't recognise was in full flow.

'Eee, I remember when she went for the motorbike test. The instructor said she had to negotiate round a set of cones in the car park. Well, she didn't stand a chance, she was all over the place. She said she felt humiliated cos the instructor was killing himself laughing and he said, "Why hinny—yu went round there like a snake with convulsions!" So she turns round to him and goes "Look! I just want to ride me bike; I divunt want to join the circus!" She was a one-off was Muriel, you can say that.'

Muriel drove mopeds and small motorbikes for years, despite having several crashes. She had hardly any vision in her right eye and, like me, she also had a bad squint. With no hope of getting a licence, she was also usually uninsured. Her system was to ride uninsured for a year, after which time she was allowed to reapply for a provisional licence for the next twelve months. Dad hated it and tried to stop her riding but this was one thing she never gave in on. She said it was a lot handier riding the bike than getting the bus. But it was evident, especially when Dad was still around, that whizzing along full throttle on her Honda 50cc, with the wind on her face, was her way of creating her own moments of freedom.

The crematorium chapel was all very congenial but there was still no vicar. Thankfully my brother is used to being on stage and didn't seem fazed.

'Right, we'll just have to do it ourselves.'

He sounded calm and confident. I followed his example and pretended I was okay. This was just like her. She always managed to embarrass me in public, even at her bloody funeral.

The funeral director, all top hat and fancy suit, agreed with my big brother.

'If you and Julie can do the eulogy between you, then I can do the committal.'

'Righto,' said my brother Trevor, with his hand on my shoulder. 'I'll kick off Julie, then you can take over. Come on, it'll be fine.'

As I followed Trevor to the front, I was struck with a paradoxical urge to pray to God for help, when in strode the vicar, adamant she was not late but that we had told her the wrong time. God is never wrong, I suppose. We had written proof that it was her mistake but perhaps in her eyes this was no more credible than the fossil record. Just something made up in an attempt to discredit Him Upstairs. Different rules were obviously at work. I hadn't offered the cake and the vicar had turned up to the funeral forty minutes late. It was cause and effect.

I used to have a little chart on my bedroom wall when I was about seven or eight. I would mark it off every day in pencil and keep it secret. It was a chart of black marks. Every time I'd done something wrong—like if I hadn't got full marks at school, or I'd stolen a bit of extra food from Mam's kitchen cupboards or answered back to my parents or brothers—I would give myself a black mark. And I'd try to get a day and even a week with no black marks, which I never managed to do. But if I *had* managed it, the war in the house would have stopped and we would all have been happy. It was cause and effect.

But I was never a good enough little girl for our family to be happy and I was too mean to give the vicar cake, so the vicar came late. I was born a sinner; and no matter how hard I work, I'll never compensate for that. It was the lies that caught me out the most, because it's wrong to tell lies and for every lie I told I'd give myself a black mark. Once my mother asked me why I was so miserable and quiet and why I refused to try some lipstick. Silence can be the most powerful sort of lie. Some bookish friends of mine now tell me that it's only ever possible to tell the real truth in fiction. But I refuse to believe them; and, because I hardly ever read novels, they think I've got a problem. But I can't see what the problem is, doggedly trying to concern myself with reality.

After the music and we'd all said our parts came the horrible bit where the coffin disappeared behind some curtains. I kind of get the metaphor, a veil between life and the hereafter maybe, but this part of the ceremony felt pathetically lame, like the truth of her being dead was being glossed over, almost sanitised. Being squeamish about death doesn't help us cope. Even the words dying, death and dead are sometimes avoided. Someone once asked when my mam had *passed*. I was tempted to explain to them that she never had the courage to even sit the motorbike test, let alone pass it.

I didn't want penny teabags and limp sandwiches for funeral food so we paid for a good lunch and bottles of fizz at a local hotel. We had Muriel's favourite treat of sherry trifle for pudding.

'Should 've had rock buns and jam tarts, Julie,' joked an old friend of hers who had the dubious pleasure, over several years, of being plied with Muriel's baking. By this time, I'd had a drink so I was free with my opinions about jam tarts.

'Her *rock buns* were bad enough; the clue was in the name. But my God, I couldn't face another jam tart in my life. Must have been responsible for a lot of dentist visits, her jam tarts. I remember my twelfth birthday. Muriel decided she would take me to Lambton Lion Park for a treat. I was on the pillion of the motorbike. I never knew that was illegal, since she didn't have a full licence, but I'm sure we shouldn't have been riding about amongst lions. She seemed to have sneaked in a back way. All the other vehicles were cars and there were big notices saying to keep moving and keep the car windows closed.

'Eee never. I can believe it though, since it's Muriel wu talkin aboot.'

'Yeah but when we got through the part with the lions we stopped for a picnic. Muriel announced she'd made some fresh jam tarts specially for my birthday. I was ready to tackle a tart when an emu started coming for me and I ran like hell. But the emu cornered me beside a little wooden hut. It was towering over me and lunging forward so I had no choice but to hoy the tart at it, hard as I could.'

'Aw bloody hell! Then what happened?'

'Well, the jam tart missed the emu but flew off like a Frisbee and the emu went legging after it and while it was distracted, I got away. Anyway, it was all alright because after it had eaten the jam tart the emu never came back.'

'Good job you're a good runner Julie, that's all I can say.'

I'd never thought of it before but not many girls from Sunderland had athletics training by trying to outrun an emu. Life with Muriel wasn't all bad.

Given my navigational record so far today has been pretty hopeless, I am beginning to doubt myself again. Have I misjudged where I came out on the road and turned in the wrong direction? I breathe a sigh of relief as two very familiar figures come into view a few hundred metres along the verge. Mandy has been scanning the fields with her binoculars. It feels like we last met in a different country, not just a few hours ago in a different county when I left the campsite this morning.

Mandy is with our friend John, who I've known since I first went to York University where he taught me statistics. John takes a deep aesthetic pleasure in mathematics, and he's a climber, mountaineer and skilled woodworker. He's also my *bezzie*, a role that has probably taxed his considerable talents more than any of life's other challenges. I learnt to rock climb with John and we have shared hundreds of adventures. He has always been around, supporting and encouraging me. As luck would have it, today is John's birthday. Mandy has saved the surprise until I get to the van. He's not one for making much of his birthdays but this is a special one. We bring out the cake, light the candles and launch into the traditional tuneless out-of-time ditty with gusto.

I was determined to make a good job of the cake, and was sent a special recipe by another York Biology graduate, Claire, who— despite having lived in America since we graduated—is still a close friend. I trust Claire in all matters of taste, and most especially culinary ones. The cake took a large amount of sweet dessert wine and is covered in grapes on top. It is a very sophisticated effort by my standards. Mandy cuts us a slice each and I'm a bit nervous, but phew—it tastes delicious. John is all smiles about the cake and we don't rush the party. But since John is joining me for the next section, we try not to pig out too much and wrap up the rest of the cake for him to take home. Once we've had a second mug of tea, it's time to get running again.

After the funeral we drove home to Cumbria in the rain, with a ramshackle arrangement of Muriel's furniture attached to the roof rack and trailer in rag-and-bone fashion. A life had been dismantled. For the next few weeks, I didn't want to see anyone or go out, even for a run, but I made myself go to work. It would have been wrong not to go to work. Otherwise, I'd sit around drinking tea and beer in my bath robe during the day, not even getting dressed, and thinking that what I had feared all my life had come to fruition, as I'd always known it would.

I used to have a piece of paper under my bed, on which I'd written in nine-year-old hand, 'It's not my fault I'm like this. I've gone mad.' For most of my childhood I had a morbid fear that I would wake one morning and not be able to speak at all, and not know who or where I was or anything about my family. This was my concept of what madness would be like. Each night I went to bed afraid I would catch madness while I was asleep, like a bad cold, and I would wake up and everyone would try treating me like normal and not understand I'd gone mad and it wasn't my fault. Now finally my girlish fears were being realised. Having conversations with my dead mother on the telephone. The phone would ring. I'd answer it and she'd speak to me, plain as day.

'Hello. Are you there, pet? When are yu cumin over, pet? Can yu bring something to prune the roses next time?'

I had never told anyone, but having unreal experiences wasn't new. For decades I would see *him* sometimes. The caravan rapist. In red-coloured trousers, with his greasy hair and pot belly. He would appear standing still and looking straight at me. He was there when I got offered my dream job teaching outdoor education in the Lake District. He was there at my graduation from medical school. The day I collected the keys for the first house I ever owned. He was present with the same physicality as anyone else, I could hear him breathing. But he never spoke. Seeing and hearing people you know are not there is disturbing because they look and sound real. But it isn't unusual, especially after trauma or during grief.

About six weeks after she died, Mam stopped talking to me— and I've never seen him again. I never *will* see him again; of that I feel confident. In the workings of my body-mind, Muriel's death removed him too. I can't tell you why this makes sense, I only feel it is so. But can you imagine, if a medical doctor had ever found out about my *symptoms*, what damage they could have wreaked? I would have been given a label, some kind of condemnation into medical madness. I would have been prescribed toxic drugs, which would have had more chance of destroying me than helping me. If I'd ever let medicine get its hands on my madness I would have been done for. Silence isn't always a method of lying; it can be a useful tool. Knowing when to keep things to myself—an invaluable lesson. And the thing about truth is, you have to understand whose truth it is. Because in reality I've never been mad, only scared. And despite all my medical training, I still fail to understand how fear can be an illness.

No Poetry

After Caleb Femi, 'Poor'

There is no poetry here, not a stanza, not a couplet, not a droplet, not like the poor poetic places where gangs of bruvers are tortured heroes risking blood in black-bladed nights, where the streets have eyes and prey on the hungry, where the next poet laureate shoplifts the dinner on their way to the library. There's nothing poetic like that here on the colourless street where the washed-out girl can't keep herself awake and she wets the bed while her mother gets fucked. See fucked, get fucked, do fucked. Where the wallpaper patterns don't join up, not a line, not a stanza, there's a ringtone and she listens on the phone and nobody's there but she hears their voices down the receiver, they curse in verse, make her feel special in the great fuzzy silence where the television talks. She is speaking to no one, she's a nutter, she's a schizo and hospital wards don't treat you with poems. There's poetic poor, then there's just poor. Poor girls pay for stuff that nobody can afford.

8 *Thin Margins*

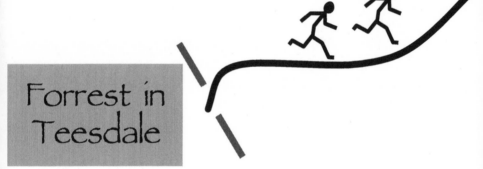

tussocks

Forrest in
Teesdale

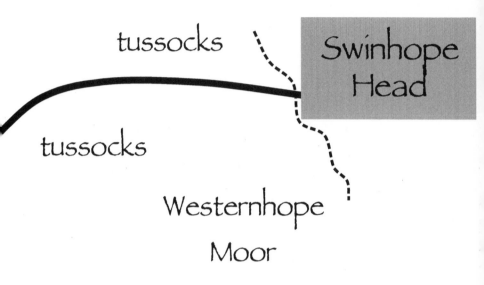

tussocks

Swinhope Head

tussocks

Westernhope Moor

Beyond any technique,
relationships are what heal.

Lewis Mehl-Madrona, Coyote Wisdom

N ovember is a time of release, a time to let go and pause and quietly anticipate the incoming tide of winter. I love the special day when the first ribbons of snow depict the topography of the fells, marking white outlines along the ridges and gullies. The Pennines are usually decorated first. Those hills are lower, but colder, than the Lakeland fells. And this particular November morning, three or four years after Muriel died, the white seemed to have come early. I hadn't yet finished looking forward to the snow before it appeared, looking rather pleased with itself, catching the first light over Cross Fell as I drove east past Penrith on my way to Melmerby, a small village in the Eden Valley. I'd been encouraged by a friend to join an Ancestors' Day, run by an American doctor who combined traditional Native American healing practices with conventional modern medicine. It turned out to be a day very different to any other I've experienced.

While I don't believe in spirits as separate entities to bodies, or an 'afterlife' in which I will have individual existence, I was still intrigued enough to come to Dr Lewis Mehl-Madrona's teaching day on ancestors. I'd greatly enjoyed his presentation on 'The Magic of Medicine' on his previous visit to the UK, and I'd been particularly impressed by his discussion of the symbolism of the stethoscope. I remembered very well how proud I had felt, as a new medical student, buying my top-of-the-range aquamarine-coloured stethoscope. I still own it and I've never used any other. I realised during Lewis's talk that it had been a kind of talisman or, as he put it, 'a magic wand'.

I'm a fully paid-up devotee of evidence-based medicine, a respectable anti-quackery kind of doctor. But I'd never use anybody else's stethoscope. It's remarkable to me that it lies quiet in its box now—after all the lungs and stomachs and hearts that have spoken through it. And the several hundred silences of dead people's chests while I have confirmed that they were indeed dead. All these sounds and silences do, in some way, feel like prayers conveyed to my ears by the blue tube. Perhaps vicars and doctors overlap—even though I hate to think so. We listen to what is inside people and make judgements about what they need. It's a delicate process and it needs a good ear.

I have met many doctors and academics who are so keen to pass on their knowledge that their teaching has an almost evangelical sermonic hardness. Lewis is a softly spoken, softly smiling man whose insights lose none of their power through his gentle delivery. In the village hall we began by drinking tea, sitting on chairs in a big circle, as low winter sunshine streamed through the full-length windows. Lewis and his partner Barbara sang an evocative Native American song and then we went around introducing ourselves and we were each asked to tell everyone something about our ancestors.

We all looked a bit dubious and one brave man articulated what many of us were thinking. 'But what if we don't like them?'

Lewis just smiled and would not be deterred.

'Well, if you keep finding ones you don't like, just look a bit harder, and find one you do. After all, we've all got so many to choose from. Two parents. Four grandparents. Eight great-grandparents. Sixteen in the next generation back. In only four generations you already have at least thirty. Then there's all the aunts and uncles and great-aunts and great-uncles and so on. Surely there's one of them you can find something to like about.'

In that moment I went from a reasoned sceptic to being like a primary school kid bursting with an answer. I was twitching in my seat as my turn approached and I just spoke what came to me without any pre-analysis.

'I have to run from my house to Gateshead as a pilgrimage to my great-grandfather. He was the founder of Gateshead Harriers. I think he died about thirty years before I was born, and this is the nearest thing I can do to meeting him. I just feel this need to connect with him and I hardly know anything about him. I've got to run Gateshead, Lewis.'

Sometimes things have a sort of emotional logic to them; and if you try and explain them in any sensible way, you're bound to fail. In a gut-felt way this ridiculous idea made total sense. American Lewis probably did not know where Gateshead was, let alone what a Harrier was in this context, and certainly wouldn't have heard of Brendan Foster or the Great North Run. But others in the group felt moved to mention that Gateshead was quite a long way from Keswick. Given my physical state, as I was trying to recover form prolapsed spinal discs and hardly able to run a step, the idea was mad; but it also made complete sense. And I felt I had no choice in it; the idea had chosen me. Was this how it felt to experience what we call destiny? Lewis didn't need to understand the particulars but understood it made sense to me, and he nodded and smiled encouragingly.

'Well, that'll be great. That'll be just great. I'll look forward to hearing all about that.'

In Native American traditions, stories are an important source of physical healing. Modern Western medicine finds a poor correlation between identifiable pathology, by which I mean the *hard* evidence of dodgy things on scans and blood tests out of range, and symptoms experienced. It deals with this by making a category of illnesses called *functional disorders*. You don't have to be a genius to realise this tactic is a sleight of hand which attempts to side-step the inadequacies of the medical model. There are times when the Western medical model of definable *organic* pathologies and targeted sophisticated treatments yields spectacular success. Which is why Lewis is a medic and uses all the tools available in his box. But still, conventional medicine persists in ignoring the complicated relationship between our body's biology and our personal experience as an inconvenient complexity. The model isn't intelligent enough to describe human health—yet. But instead of changing the model, we tend to vilify people whose pain is not justified by *identifiable pathology*. Western medicine has yet to develop the intelligence to deal with whole stories. It's like trying to write something meaningful using only the mechanics of words and grammar, with no access to simile, metaphor or plot, not to mention poetry.

Each of our lives is a story, intertwined with others' stories, and to what extent we write our own script—that's intriguing. It partly depends on how much attention we pay to the story we are living out, and how much we are willing to question it. Changing our stories doesn't always have to involve grand transformations. I once saw someone turn a shopping list into a beautiful poem. But it still functioned as a shopping list. The magical power of stories is that the particulars can remain very similar, but the meaning can be wholly different, depending on the way it's told.

In my story, family was something to be endured where necessary and escaped from where possible. The way I looked at it, life was a quest to reform everything that was wrong with me; and my family were there to disrupt the plot and drag me back into the stew of shame. I had yet to grasp how deeply flawed this telling of my story was, on many levels. But by the time I left the Ancestors'

Day at Melmerby, I was a woman on a mission, determined to find out about Jack Nowell; and surely there must be lots to find out. After all, he founded one of the most influential athletics clubs in British history. And at that moment, although it was a daunting prospect, I was also determined to find a way to run to Gateshead.

'The next bit looks tricky on the map, John. Getting up to the moor.'

'I've got it waymarked on the phone. We can use that.'

I'm a proud Luddite when it comes to electronic navigation, but I try and look appreciative of John's kindness. We set off up a steep lane past a few cottages, me with map in hand and John with phone in pocket. I'm in front but I soon stop, unsure of where to go as the tarmac runs out.

'Should be a stile, or a gate or something. We need to be in that field, I think. No sign of a path though, but there is one on the map.'

John gets out his phone, types in his password, waits for the map to load, then agrees. I'm sceptical about why the map on the phone is more reliable than the one in my hand—it's certainly a lot trickier to look at. But John explains it can zoom into details as well as tracking exactly where we are, which seems reassuring and oddly disappointing at the same time. I love the business of matching map to landscape and I don't want to lose that skill, which—on the evidence of the last couple of days—is already getting rusty.

We climb over a gate tied up with string and find a vague path on the other side. After a couple more fields, we notice an old footpath sign on a stone. A faded arrow in a circle on the next gate encourages us to trot on further, even though the gate doesn't open. After several more fields there's no knowing where we are. I only have a 1:50,000 scale Ordnance Survey map for this route, as anything on a bigger scale would have been just too much map, and it doesn't have walls and fences marked.

'I'll get the phone out.'

Same palaver—password, wait for the orbiting satellites to tune in, etc.

'Where are we then?'

A few minutes standing looking for clues while I wait for John to get the better of the gadget.

'No reception. The map's on the screen though. Come and have a look.'

I peer at the screen out of courtesy but can't see much in the bright sunshine. I remind myself that, as annoying as I find the phone, it is a useful idea, and John is here out of the goodness of his heart, to help me. But over an hour after eating the cake and leaving Mandy we are still lost in a maze of fields and it's hot and frustrating and I just want to make progress.

'Hang on. Got some reception. Oh look. We need to be miles over there to the right.'

'Yes, I thought that from the map but none of the paths seem to actually exist.'

I'd anticipated a pleasant run through the countryside, not a stop-start maunder through squares of grass penned in by walls we couldn't see over. After another age of messing about, when we sometimes seem to be going in circles, we come to a path. The path leads over a stream and up past a lone, white-painted house with washing on the line.

'Good drying day,' I remark, smiling to myself. A little homage to Muriel, who had a stock of favourite phrases which her children collected for amusement.

Part of me wishes I could still hear her voice properly, disconcerting as it was.

The house and stream are on the map and happily we are back on track. After a lot of fiddling with string-tied gates and figuring out where exactly to go next, we follow another vague trod up a narrow grassy slope, with a tall drystone wall a metre to our left, and the stream just to the right, running in a deep-cut ravine lined with thickets of brambles and gorse. One thing about John is that you hardly ever hear him shout. He's not a shouty kind of person. I am looking at the stream, hoping we won't need to go through the spiky vegetation to cross it, when I hear John scream, 'Get to the wall!'

Without looking, I leap leftwards instantly, my heart nearly coming through my ribs. I'm like a Tom and Jerry character plastered to the drystone wall, which is taller than me, attempting to make myself two-dimensional. John is my cartoon buddy stuck to the wall next to me, as a huge black and white cow comes steaming down the path. The ground is shaking, and after she's passed us, we can't stop shaking either. The beast had intent. There was no doubt—she was charging for us. But the great bulk of her had such momentum that she couldn't stop or change course, so she missed us by inches. Being gored by a cow is a horrific thing which does happen to several people every year in the British countryside, sometimes fatally. Being gored by a cow on your birthday, when you've only come out to help a friend... As Muriel would say—'it doesn't bear thinking about'.

For a few minutes we are stuck there, afraid to move, in case the beast comes back. With fugitive vigilance we tiptoe onwards and over a stile at the top of the hill, out onto the moor. We've only made about four miles progress since leaving Mandy but we've been going for nearly two hours. She'll probably be at the next road crossing, wondering where we are. Alarmed at the reminder of how thin the margins are between us and oblivion, we try to put it all behind us and break into a slow run.

I had visions of running from home to Gateshead without stopping at all. For most ultra-distance runners this would not be such a big task. Running, though, is not simply a mind-over-matter affair. You do need the bones and muscles and nerves and blood and lungs and heart for it. I was frustrated because I still had huge pain where I had broken my sacrum and pelvis. I imagined I would heal quickly but it can take several years, of patient exercises and strengthening and massage, for healing to take place. And it has taken me such a long time to learn that bullying my tissues is counterproductive.

I'm learning to approach my body the way I approach my garden. It needs a lot of work and tending, but it has its own organic way of flourishing when given the right conditions. A plant will grow when nurtured, but if it's forced then it's weak and vulnerable. The Buddhist teacher Tara Brach says that life is not a matter of survival of the fittest, but survival of the nurtured. My plan was to start doing some slow, gentle runs and just build up time on my feet, even if I had to walk sometimes. I realised this run would be about distance, not hills. I was used to keeping track of the amount of work I did by thinking of metres of ascent and descent. Now I'd have to get used to covering miles on paths, rather than ups and downs on rough fells. So I started with some flatter outings, beginning with runs around Derwentwater from my house. And I also started finding out about Jack Nowell. And, as it turned out, neither of these was easy.

Family history was the very last thing I thought I would ever be interested in researching. Muriel had told me some snippets but mostly when I was little. As a teenager and adult, I closed my ears. I didn't want to know about her sadness. How she had loved her mother, Maggie. How her mother had played the piano and taught her the names of flowers and then died when Mam was eleven. I was much younger than eleven when she started telling me. I have vague memories of feeling very cold when she told me the story of her mother being 'taken ill'.

Mam was sent to her Aunty Dinah's house not far away. Then, two days later, Dinah told her that her mam had died of pneumonia. As a child I didn't know how to react to Mam's story. I saw it in my mind in black and white. Maybe because her old photographs were in black and white. The whole thing seemed so far removed from me. If only I could have my mam back for a day, just to get the story straight. But even if I could, I still wouldn't get the story straight. Because if I ever asked a question, Muriel never answered it directly. She was oddly evasive. She'd move on to something different.

I thought maybe she was stupid, that it was impossible to have a proper conversation with her. That she was incapable of listening to my questions and just wanted to have a sounding board for the bits she wanted to say out loud. I was a kid, this was a story; I wanted a story I could follow, that made sense. I didn't understand why people told parts of stories and went to their graves leaving so much untold. I wasn't even old enough to understand why I kept my own secrets. I was a poor counsellor, and it didn't occur to me there could be reasons why she missed out the parts that had been locked away. Reasons like trauma, pain, shame, grief, anger, heartbreaking disappointment and even guilt. And I had no idea that

Mam's childhood experiences could possibly have an influence on my own physical body.

It isn't all just chance—the things we find out about and the things we close our ears to. A few years ago, I was on a train to London from Penrith, on my way to a conference on 'Food as Medicine'. At that time this whole field of treating specific illnesses with specific diets was something most of my medical colleagues found hard to swallow, despite humans having over two thousand years of knowledge on the subject. Certain kinds of knowledge are not permissible. It grieves me that huge amounts of medical herbal knowledge were lost in the European witch hunts that took place in the fourteenth to the seventeenth centuries. Sometimes some of this wisdom is now rediscovered as *science*. What we choose to know about at any one time has as much to do with cultural power politics as it is does with any concept of *objective science*. Traditional feminine knowledge, of plants and food and health—that's not very cutting edge. A medical consultant in my study group told me they understood the general concept of a healthy diet, but they couldn't believe that certain illnesses could actually be treated by certain foods. But I was on the train to London to discover more of the *evidence*.

On the journey I was reading a book called *The Epigenetics Revolution*, when by complete coincidence a doctor I knew happened to get on and sat down opposite. He wasn't going to the conference but we chatted and he noticed my book.

'What's epigenetics?'

'Well, it's all about how other molecules attach themselves to DNA and switch our genes on and off. Say, for example, during starvation a load of genes are activated and others are inactivated, in the body's effort to conserve energy and essential functions. But some of these changes seem to persist even if food becomes available again. The most surprising thing is that some of these modifications stuck onto DNA, and affecting the function of the genes, can be passed from parent to offspring. So stuff that happens to our parents and grandparents during their lifetimes can be passed down to us, through our genes.'

'Sounds like Lamarck to me. Thought he was discredited by Darwin long ago. Must be some pseudoscientific nonsense surely.'

'Well, I don't think so. The author, Nessa Carey, is a senior lecturer in molecular biology at Imperial College London. I reckon her work is robust and peer reviewed and all that. I can lend it to you if you want. Anyhow, this epigenetics stuff's been all over the place. Don't you read *New Scientist*, or the paper, or listen to Radio 4?'

After a bit more chat about something we had in common—fell racing—and about how he reckoned he could do a road marathon any day of the week without any training, because fell races were much harder, I settled back down to the book. It was tricky. Full of technical details about genes and their mechanisms. How they get switched on and off or are 'expressed' or stay silent. The stories that do and don't get told are inside our cells too. You can inherit a gene but it has no effect unless it gets switched on.

I wanted to race through the book and find out about this Lamarck idea, epitomised in the schoolbook example of the story of how giraffes got long necks. Did this science of epigenetics somehow vindicate the ideas of Lamarck that were so derided in my education in favour of those of Darwin? Carey never mentioned giraffes but she did talk about how genes are altered as a result of the experiences of the organisms they belong to, and how these changes can be passed on. There are lots of caveats, and this is a new science with a lot still to understand and be curious about. Epigenetic effects are real but we don't yet know how important they are in our lives. It's likely the effects are subtle and may not play a major role in health. And just because Lamarck may have been a little bit right does not mean Darwin was in the least bit wrong. It turns out Darwin was extra right because he said his ideas and Lamarck's ideas were both valid. They were not opposed to one another. There can be more than way of being right.

Darwin was willing to accept the complexity of more than one model operating together. But we like a story with a good guy and a bad guy, or a smart one and a stupid one, and we like heroes. Darwin was a clever man, no doubt about that, but his work followed on from the work of others at the time and was part of a cultural shift. His theory of natural selection didn't come out of the blue. If Darwin was a genius, it was because he unified certain lines of existing enquiry into a useful model of evolution, and it was also because he knew that all knowledge is provisional. The bank is tangled, the complexity of the natural world is a story without an end.

Gazing out of the train window, as intimate glimpses of anonymous back gardens and allotments flitted by, I wondered what all this epigenetics stuff meant. My mam's mam dying like that, and then, soon after, my mam being a war evacuee without enough to eat and no love, and separated from her two younger siblings who she felt responsible for—is any of that written in the language of my own epigenetics? Strange ideas these, and against everything I had been taught as a genetics student and everything I wanted to believe.

My life was about me writing on my own blank slate. Not only did the past not concern me, I also actively wanted to block it out. But what if I couldn't? I started Googling articles on epigenetics and intergenerational trauma. What if my feeling so vulnerable was biological and not just a product of my upbringing? My mind was spinning with related thoughts. It seemed that neither of my parents had been nurtured, and that they were both haunted by past traumas. I had my own ghosts to contend with, but I had hoped that, with help and love and commitment to the cause of freeing myself, I could be liberated from the shame and hurt, the anger and self-disgust, I often felt mired in. But what if these things were so intrinsic to my biology that they couldn't be changed?

There is something mesmeric about gazing from a moving train and gradually my distressing thoughts began to settle. If it is true that the sufferings of our parents and grandparents can affect our own biology then whole generations of the downtrodden and persecuted must be affected. Do all us Geordies and Mackems bear the scars of the unemployment and starvation which led to the Jarrow March in 1936? Do all the children of those who had a difficult war carry inherited sadness? Then I thought about the millions of African descendants of the enslaved. The experiences of our ancestors affect us, of course. They affect our cultural identity, our stories, our language and our ways of life.

Until this 'Epigenetics Revolution', the popular scientific view was that genetics was a one-way street. Our genes affect our lives but our lives don't change our genes. In an ecosystem purely driven by natural selection, it was simply a case of those with less favourable genes dying out. In this way, the environment influences the species as a whole by selecting who will survive, but the environment doesn't change the genes of an individual. But with these new insights about epigenetics, everything seemed a lot trickier and messier.

The beautiful simplicity of Darwin's model, which felt secure and inscrutable when I was nestled in the University Library in York, was no longer so straightforward. Yes Mr Darwin, we oversimplified you. Life is messy, and complicated. The train slowed down as it passed rows of neat gardens, with lawns and borders and carefully pruned roses. I wondered where this association between neatness and beauty came from. I found the asking of this question suddenly emancipating. Mess can be beautiful. Even Einstein struggled with the deeply chaotic nature of nature. But the association of order with beauty was only ever an idea. Just an idea that helps us control life, but not any kind of truth. The poet John Keats famously asserted that 'truth is beauty'. He didn't say anything about order being beautiful.

I gave up reading, it was hard work, and just enjoyed gazing aimlessly out of the window. My doctor friend put down his running magazine to go to the buffet car.

'Don't suppose you'll want a coffee, Julie? Probably too unhealthy for you?'

'Oh, coffee would be great. I'll have a large cappuccino with chocolate on. Good for the brain—coffee, and chocolate. It's all in the literature.'

When I got home after the conference, I was still grappling with the epigenetics book and still searching for information about Jack Nowell. He must be *in the literature* too. It would be a question of knowing where to look.

There is a certain type of ground much hated by fellrunners because it's not only totally impossible to run on, it also takes enormous effort, and a very odd gait, to even walk over. This is tussock. What we call *babies' heads*. If the runner puts a foot on the tussock, it will not support their weight and the tussock will slump over. The leg slips sideways, wrenching the ankle, and the runner usually ends up lying on the ground in a twisted position which is very hard to get up from. If the foot is put between the tussocks there is more chance of staying upright but you tend to sink down into a mire of wetness underneath the matted grasses. Then it's very hard work to pull the foot back up to take the next step, and the leg has to be lifted an awful long way up to clear the next tussock. Occasionally there are deeper, unseen holes between the tussocks, and the runner goes in knee deep, then sinks forward and head butts the ground in front. The ground at least has the decency to be soft, even though the grasses can be sharp enough to cut bare skin.

The moor up from Teasdale to Swinhope Head is the most perfect example of this type of ground I have ever come across. Classic *babies' heads*, uphill, in over 20 degrees and blazing sun, on already tired legs. At least I am with John, though I can't help feeling sorry for him spending his birthday like this. I suppose the other good thing is that the aggressive cow is still down near the stream and can't get up onto the moor. This route is marked on the map as part of a long-distance path called 'A Pennine Journey'.

'Fancy if you saw this on a map and thought it would make a nice walk for a holiday and booked some B and Bs. That would be terrible, wouldn't it?'

John laughs at my joke. As if anyone would do that. Who would want to come here on their holidays? It's almost the definition of barren. But as we plod on, we notice there are larks, and more and more larks. And we begin to quite enjoy the sunshine and the clear air and the absence of anything else. No traffic noise—no sound at all, except the birds. No change in the view, just the same pale-brown moor ahead. Not even a cloud. It's a type of minimalism. In fact, I begin to think that tussock trudging could be seen as the purest of performing arts. The whole thing becomes quite mesmerising, and time no longer seems to matter.

Every now and then, we think we've spied a thin trod of a path. But they soon peter out. It is one of those experiences a certain type of person might describe as mindful, but in fact it's utterly mindless. The knowledge that we are still only progressing at a snail's pace is irrelevant, since no more effort can be applied. We are doing our best and sooner or later we will arrive at Swinhope Head. Surely.

Uneducated as I am, it isn't until the following week that I find out about 'A Pennine Journey'. This route is based on a walk taken by Alfred Wainwright in 1938. After first writing my own account, I was amused to find out how my fumbling feet contrasted with Wainwright's more adept technique. AW described how, when walking over the moor to Swinhope Head, your feet become 'the centre of your little world' and you watch them walking 'left, right, left, right' and he wondered what would happen if they went 'left, right, left, left, right' instead. I can tell you AW, what would happen—you would fall over ungracefully. But you seem to have been incapable of such inefficiency, since you continue by saying that despite exerting all your willpower to 'make them blunder' they keep going in an orderly fashion. Hence your conclusion that their actions are not controlled by the brain but are automatic. And so

> *'you pause to wipe your glasses and look about you for the hundredth time, quite uselessly. [...] No other type of holiday could have induced such a feeling of severance from the familiar; it is a change complete...'*

Next time you're looking for something a bit different to do on your holidays, try going over the moor to Swinhope Head.

Mandy has driven up the narrow tarmac road which winds its way over Westernhope Moor, forming a snaky link between Teesdale in Yorkshire and Weardale in County Durham. John and I can see the van perched up on the crest of the hill above us like a little toy, which never seems to get any bigger. On my schedule I'd estimated an hour and ten minutes for this section but we've already taken over twice as long. Mandy picks up two little people in the binoculars and wonders what can be slowing us down so much. There's only a few hundred more metres of tussock dancing and we pick up the hint of a grassy track and the going improves.

When Alfred Wainwright came this way, it was also September and, like now, 'Fear and apprehension prevailed through the country.' The context of his holiday was the imminent Second World War. Wainwright describes how:

> *'The newspaper headings appeared in larger and larger and blacker and blacker type; their effect was to stun you so that you read on in a state of torpor, which in turn gave way to extreme nervous debility; you couldn't get things in proper perspective at all with those screaming headlines searing into your brain.'*

Until six months ago I wouldn't have been able to empathise, but now I know only too well what AW is talking about. The trance of being addicted to the media, then during the Munich Crisis, and now during the Covid pandemic; wanting not to listen but being drawn into repetitive and terrifying *news*. He even describes how novel words and phrases dominated everyday language:

> *'Fortifications, dugouts, plebiscites, armaments, bomb-proof shelters, decontamination squads, conscription, incendiary bombs, Air-raid precautions...'*

The lexicon of a crisis fuels our fears: social distancing, PCR, lateral flow, R-number, ventilators, PPE, shielding, self-isolating, daily briefing, COBRA committee, follow the science, spike protein, new variant, herd immunity, remote learning, Zooming…

It's poignant and sad to read about Wainwright's fears of war, yet he gives me hope that all this virus-speak will also one day fade into bad memories. I know I'd be naive to think that events such as wars and pandemics don't reverberate into the decades which follow. But meanwhile, just as AW did, I find peace up on the 'wild Pennine hills' where 'the larks sang their heart out'.

Arriving at the van, we are hot and tired and in disbelief at how much five miles can take out of you. Mind you, we are still alive— uncrushed by our bovine would-be assailant. I wonder if I should tell Mandy about the cow. What with yesterday's electrocution, she might start losing confidence that I'm going to get to Gateshead alive after all.

'Are you alright? Seems to have taken you ages that. Tea? Kettle's boiled.'

'Ah, yes please Mandy. But water as well. Cold water. Can't believe it's this hot in September.'

John looks relieved that we've made the rendezvous and doesn't mention our near-death encounter.

'Well, I won't forget this birthday in a hurry. Great way to spend it. I think I'll go a different way back to the car though.'

And so we part company again. John heading back to Teesdale, Mandy heading down the road to Weardale in the van, and me taking on the next section of moor alone—and this time there isn't even a path on the map.

Revision

Lehninger—Principles of Biochemistry was always my favourite book
classy and smooth, smelling of knowledge, every line and equation
perfectly structured molecular syntax and diction, the narrative
was out of this world, beyond all blurbs, how extraordinary—
the peerless genius of a ribosome. The matchless matrix of mitochondria
linking a chain of electron transport, stream of consciousness
the eloquent erudition of it all—substrate, enzyme, life.

To be is to be catalysed,

　　　　　　　　dissolved, evaporated, solidified.

Lehninger—you gave me everything I needed, that first intimacy
sitting in silence by the library window. I was so taken,
like a salvation.

9 Nurture Changes Nature

Black Hill

Swinhope Head

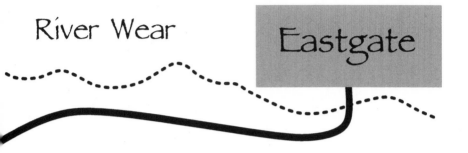

River Wear

Eastgate

Sometimes the greatest scientific
breakthroughs happen because someone
ignores the prevailing pessimism.

Nessa Carey, The Epigenetics Revolution

A hundred and fifty years ago, in the name of science, a man chopped the tails of mice and found those mice had babies with tails as good and strong as any other healthy mice. The brutal experience of the parent mice at the hands of the human experimenter had not transferred to their genes which programmed the growth of their babies' tails. In my genetics lectures at university this experiment was cited as proof that Lamarck was one hundred per cent wrong, in every case.

And giraffes? It's like Darwin said: the ones with the genes for longer necks get more food, grow healthy and strong, and so have more little giraffes and pass those long-neck genes on. The short-neck giraffes are not as well adapted and are poorly nourished. They can't have many healthy babies and so their short-neck genes die out, and the whole giraffe community stands tall. But evolution is not only about Darwinian survival of the fittest. The experiment with the mice tails wasn't the end of the story of 'the inheritance of acquired characteristics'. Epigenetics can tweak things in subtle ways, perhaps not as evident as tail or no-tail. For example, childhood trauma can leave a person vulnerable for a long time, perhaps their whole lives. Nessa Carey says that's in part because being scared when we are little turns on the genes for responding to stress, so we have more cortisol and other edgy hormones coursing about. And sometimes the genes don't get turned off and can be more easily activated for a few generations.

Is it a good thing for humanity that I never had kids? Maybe only good, calm people should breed. Carey does not say that, and certainly does not support any unsavoury ideas about selective breeding in humans. But she did propose a mechanism for how a tendency towards anger and aggression can be partly inherited, at least in mice. She told a story about two mice who were down the pub. One mouse spilled the other mouse's pint of beer and Carey speculated on which genes would need to be active in the aggrieved mouse for this situation to degenerate into a fight. Professor Carey obviously spends an awful lot of time thinking about genes, but when it comes to our DNA and our behaviour there are many other things to consider. For instance, regardless of which genes were at play, it could make a difference if the mouse with spilt beer was rich and could get another round in with no money worries, or if it was church-poor and that was the only pint it had managed to buy for several weeks.

Although scientists employ stories to communicate, science purports to use a different set of methods from those of storytelling; but both are endeavours concerned with cause and effect. Variations on simplistic stories about how genes dictate behaviour frequently pop up in the media. So-called 'warrior genes' and 'happiness genes' have been cited as examples, respectively making people aggressive or contented. When it comes down to it, the scientific basis for these is very sketchy indeed, with small statistical differences being overblown into proven causal mechanisms. Am I a good runner because I possess what has been described as the 'running gene', passed down from Jack Nowell? No. There are no such things as running genes; I wish it were that simple. Complex traits, like athleticism, depend on a myriad of variables, not just a handful of genes. And our complex emotions and behaviours can be influenced by our genes, but certainly not dictated by them as media spins sometimes suggest.

When we first learn about genes at school, the usual starting point is to take a trait like eye colour and explain it in terms of the blue-eye brown-eye dichotomy. The brown gene is dominant over the blue. We have two copies of most of our genes within the nuclei of our cells—one from each parent. The brown-eye gene being dominant will trump the blue gene, so if we have one copy of each gene, we will have brown eyes. To have blue eyes, we need two blue genes so both parents must carry that gene. Those parents might still have brown eyes themselves, if they have one blue, one brown gene. But we can't have blue eyes unless both parents have at least one blue gene, even if it's not evident by looking at them.

It's a really neat model, and therein lies the problem. It's amazing how many children will swallow this theory, while being aware that they only have to look around them and see all kinds of different eye colours in their classmates. I do wonder why we are so gullible and fall for the easy story when all around us things don't match that simplicity. There are actually at least eight genes which influence eye colour and some environmental factors too. And as you will have observed, there are lots of different eye colours.

Imagine how much more fraught with difficulty it is to talk about traits like athleticism and intelligence and emotional wisdom, which are influenced by thousands of our genes and thousands of events in our lives. Although we all have some common understanding of what we mean when we discuss such traits, they are complex qualities which are very hard to measure with any accuracy. Then layer on the fact that I'm only athletic when I train to be so, and I'm only intelligent when I have the wisdom to use my intelligence. So often, when held in the grip of strong emotions or a simple story in which I have a vested interest, I have become utterly stupid. Even when we are capable of expressing certain traits, they are not all fixed and our ability to express them can wax and wane depending on circumstance.

This is a gamble. I am cutting the corner off Wainwright's 'Pennine Journey' route. Instead of taking the sinuous road down into Weardale, I head straight out over Black Hill. There are many *Black Hills* in the Pennines. Many dark invitations for the legs to be immersed in peat. I'm surprised nobody has marketed peat hag tramping as a kind of therapy or beauty treatment. A mind-body detoxification experience. This Black Hill is more golden and glowing in the afternoon sunshine and has little exposed peat to contend with. It's a bit tussocky but not too bad and very runnable, even without a defined trod.

I am constantly scanning and choosing the best-looking line and slightly adjusting as the vegetation varies. This is all I have to do. Just run. And enjoy these sunny moments of freedom up here in my red-and-white vest. I'm heading almost north and pick up a fence line which merges into a drystone wall, forming a spine along the top of a broad ridge. I pass a little reedy pool and slow down to take in the view. The country is open and expansive, and the sky is big. I open my ears but can hear almost nothing. Everything is quiet and blissfully wide and peaceful. I feel expanded and time feels infinite.

Still following the wall, I pass the high point of the moor with its sturdy trig point, and a thin path develops. I like this kind of running, where there is no marked path on the map to create expectations, and I also like running with no luggage. Because of Mandy's support and the kind weather, I can be up here in shoes, socks, shorts and a vest, carrying only a tiny bum-bag with a windproof top and a phone.

I sometimes feel horrified, especially when out in winter, by all my *kit*. Expensive shoes, special insoles and socks, base layers and insulated layers, a couple of changes of gloves and hat, breathable waterproofs, a lightweight rucksack, emergency shelter, first aid, food, a flask, compass, map, phone. I can easily go out the door with a few hundred quids' worth. And when I go climbing, add in ropes and gear and harness and helmet, and maybe ice axes and crampons, and we are into thousands. The way I interact with the outdoors is not exactly *free*. The biggest change I've seen in terms of kit and running is the emergence of a *trail running* market, which seems to be a genre of running somewhat driven by the people who sell kit. Recently I went to our local shop to replace my twenty-year-old running rucksack (to my shame, because it could possibly be repaired). Trying on a bag laden with straps and pockets, I asked my friend the shopkeeper, 'What's this for, Chris?'

'It's to put your poles in, I think. You know, then you can have that *trail runner look*.'

Immediately we shared a mental picture of a long-socked, double-shorted, peak-capped, pole-propelled runner with various tubes and bottles sticking out from their luggage.

'No, that's not really you though, is it Jules?'

We shared a knowing laugh. Enough said. I bought the rucksack because it was comfortable on my back. My friend is a master of his craft—knowing his customers.

This is nothing like Wainwright's approach. He carried almost nothing, except spare socks and a cape. He ate breakfast and dinner at lodgings and didn't carry food during the day. He would probably consider me a glutton, stopping for all the drinks and snacks that Mandy provides. He usually covered between two and two and a half miles per hour, and many days was out for ten or twelve hours. As so-called runners, John and I didn't go much faster than AW's pace on the previous section. But we'd given up the idea of running then really.

And now, the way across Black Hill is easier. I'm enjoying being back in a trotting rhythm, picking my way through the grassy moorland, and it isn't even all that boggy. It's lovely. With this being a grouse moor, I've been worried about coming across an angry gamekeeper who doesn't want me up here. I'm not good with confrontation and usually either get hopelessly angry or crumble into silent acquiescence. Nonviolent communication and assertiveness—I know the principles. But both fear and anger are switches which turn off reason. So, I'm working on it. I even rehearse a little polite but assertive speech in my head, in case I get chased.

'Oh, I'm terribly sorry but I did check on the map and under the Countryside and Rights of Way Act (CROW Act) of 2000 this land appears to designated as *open access land*. I'm planning to run north down this hill to meet a public footpath going into the valley. Okay.'

But I don't meet a gamekeeper, friendly though they might have been anyway. I meet nobody. I am gloriously alone. The ground steepens but the running stays easy, on a soft grassy path that merges into a quad bike track. I can see Weardale wending below me, and I can see the path through the patchwork of drystone walls at the bottom of the hill. I'm just running, easily and freely. Across the other side of the valley is another wide horizon of moorland with a slightly purplish heathery haze. There are trees in the bottom, down by the river, so the colourscape from bottom to top is deep green, golden green, brown, purple, blue. A blue so big and bright I begin to question if I am really in the English Pennines. This time yesterday I was plagued with pain in my lower back and pelvis. But now I'm just running over soft ground, down an ever-steepening hill into Weardale. Source of my home river.

The River Wear runs on, to emerge in Sunderland where its moorland water slakes the sea.

I finished Professor Carey's excellent book and did something I thought I'd never do. I went on an ancestry website. I thought all this ancestry business was a stupid waste of time, and a deluded way of seeking self-importance. Being related to royalty, for example, is no big deal, considering that we all are. But not everyone is delighted to discover that *every human who was alive only five thousand years ago with present-day living relatives is an ancestor of all eight billion of us.*

It's not that there was only one ancestral Adam and Eve five thousand years ago but that family trees never branch neatly. They also join and cross and become entangled with one another in ever-diverging lineages. Humanity is a closely matted web and nobody has a claim to be more special than anyone else, either culturally or genetically. And I always thought seeking ancestral connections was tied up in a very hierarchical status-driven view of the world. Surely we should exist by our own efforts and not resort to some vicarious sense of inherited pride for our personal significance. Above all, being interested in my ancestry seemed inherently middle class. In some paradoxical way it affronted my inherited working-class sensibilities.

I was shocked at myself. How could I go on an ancestry website? These websites seem like some ludicrous interpretation of how genetics actually works—or doesn't work. The marketing of this multi-billion-dollar industry promises individuals that they can uncover insights into their heritage by genetic testing. While gene testing can uncover a very broad sense of the geographical homes of recent ancestors, there are usually no surprises in most people's gene tests. I am part Viking, part Celt, part Anglo-Saxon. I know this because my genetic heritage is very likely be roughly the same as almost every other person of northern European descent. I don't need a test to tell me.

People sometimes get gene tests because they are searching for close family relatives, and gene testing does sometimes succeed in throwing up matches and allowing estranged relatives to connect. However, genetic concepts of race and ethnicity are deeply flawed. There are no defined genetic dividing lines between different human populations. With the rare exceptions of remote indigenous groups, there just hasn't been enough isolation of most populations, especially in the last millennia or two, for our family trees to be separate lineages. The lines keep merging back with each other. We are not a tree but a tapestry. Yet even Darwin was scared to challenge wrong-headed popular concepts of race in human biology, remarking: 'I think I shall avoid the whole subject as it is so surrounded in prejudices.'

There is no doubt though that Darwin was a radical who did pose a huge challenge to the idea that humans were created separately from animals, in the image of God. He may have been reluctant to admit it but in the end the evidence he had amassed pointed to only one conclusion—that there had been a lineage of species through evolution and we had 'descended' from other apes. I find it vaguely amusing, given the social stigma attached to our now extinct relatives the Neanderthals, who have been unfairly trolled as stupid and thuggish, that there is more Neanderthal DNA in the world now than when these relatives of ours were alive. Most of us have between 0.5 and 2 per cent Neanderthal DNA, due to interbreeding in the distant past. No need to be ashamed of it either, since, contrary to common belief, these cousins had significantly bigger brains than us on average. This begs the question: who were really the brutes?

Modern genetic science is uncompromising on the matter—two black people are as likely to be genetically different to each other as a black person and a white person. There is much more variation within groups than between groups. The concept of *race* in the human species is largely a social construct and not a genetic reality. Darwin was a supporter of the abolition of slavery and seemed to understand our common humanity, but his theory of evolution by natural selection was misappropriated in the late 1800s by a Victorian imperialist elite with their own social agenda.

Darwin's cousin, Francis Galton, came up with the term 'eugenics' to popularise the notion that human society could be improved by selective breeding. The fact that genes do not determine very much about social behaviour has not stopped the bigotry of the white supremacist movement whose supporters fear that 'lower races' will 'replace' them. Those who identify as ethnically white are not the icing on the cake of humanity—simply an ingredient mixed in with all the others. We all know the logical conclusion of twentieth-century delusions about genetics and race. Seventeen million of these conclusions: Jews, Roma people, the emotionally unwell and physically disabled, homosexuals, dissidents, Soviets and Slavs were murdered by various means, including gas chambers, forced labour and starvation, during the Second World War. And many, many more made into refugees, with everything, except their dignity, destroyed or stolen. They were all our family; every single one of them. Tribal violence is humanity's central problem and we are not showing any signs of evolving out of it. We don't need to change our genes to do this—we need to change our stories.

Coming along a farm track to meet the tiny tarmac road, I turn right and see our van squeezed into a lay-by. It's hot down here in the valley and I'm in need of a drink. Mandy and I don't say much. It feels too peaceful to break the atmosphere with conversation. I take water and point to a spot on the map on the other side of the river, near a church, for our next meeting. Now I have a couple of miles on the road but it's a small road lined with big trees which are kind enough to shade me for a while. There are no cars but I can hear the river off to my left. I'm on tarmac again. I'm trying not to dislike the tarmac but it's hot, and the familiar tension and pain is creeping into my sinews.

It doesn't mean much, this pain. I've come to realise that. It's a kind of learned response in my tissues but it doesn't signal anything useful. If I were to tear a muscle or put my foot down a hole and break my ankle, the pain would stop me, hopefully, and protect me. But this everyday torture doesn't do that. It just moans on, like an ungrateful child in a crabby mood. It's not got anything useful to say. Like an irked parent trying to be patient, I tell my body it's doing well. It's a good body, it's valued and listened to. Yes, pain, I hear you, but you can relax, I've heard you. I set up this internal dialogue and try to visualise the comfort and ease and freedom of movement I had on the moor. It sort of helps, a bit.

I can hear the River Wear flowing and gurgling. It's a small river, about 15 feet wide, and shallow, overhung with thick trees, all dappled and lovely. I'm listening and there's not much movement in the leaves, not much breeze, just water flowing over rocks and the plaintive call of a buzzard winging high overhead in the cloudless blue sky. I am trying to imagine what the buzzard is seeing. Is it looking at me? What does it think? How does it sense where its feathers are on its wing tips? Does it feel scary up there?

There's a kind of drowsiness to the heat and I almost feel like I need a nap. But I'd better wake up, as there's a main road to cross and a bit of mapwork to figure out. I pull my sweaty little piece of OS map out of my crop-top and it suggests there's a path down to a bridge, leading to the end of the Weardale railway line and the village of Eastgate. It all looks very vague in practice, and I notice a sign saying 'No Access Across River', so I continue on the deserted road for a few hundred yards and turn left down to the metal road bridge over to the main A698. The river is shifting in a shallow steady flow of translucent brown, flecked with floating leaves and a few white feathers. The mighty River Wear that has launched tens of thousands of ships over eight hundred years. Up here it's a sleepy little river in a land that time forgot.

The main road soon smashes my serenity as I dodge the traffic to cross—and pass a bus shelter with a note about it being the site of a Roman altar to Sylvanus, god of the woods and hunting. Apparently the shrine was erected by a Roman calvary commander to give thanks for the hunting down of a very large wild boar. It must have been a fabulous hunting ground this. The village is called Eastgate because it was the east gate of the second-largest hunting estate in England in the 1400s. It was private of course, *belonging* to the Prince Bishops of Durham. Commoners like me would have been excluded.

This appropriation of land by powerful gentry in England has been the ruin of the place. At least with the Countryside and Rights of Way Act of 2000 we have been granted a certain amount of access. The white English aristocracy really have done a job, not only on plundering and robbing people of other skin colours from other countries but also on the people of their own lands and on the land itself. When I was a teenager, I would feel a strong sense of trespass as I rode my bike out of our estate and into the countryside. Like I did not belong there or have a right to such places. Now I'm invested with the spirit of Henry Irwin Jenkinson of Latrigg and I begin to feel the resilience of my working-class heritage. I have one of Dougie MacLean's songs in my head, with the line saying that you can't own the land because the land owns you.

The road noise is messing up my brain but I find the lane up past the church where Mandy will be waiting. I'm a bit weary again now and I feel like yesterday was months ago.

Exploring my close family roots became very tricky. I was emotionally drawn in—but I was suspicious of myself. Was I trying to lay a false claim to something? Was I being emotionally hijacked by pseudoscience suggesting that the spurious notion of being a *good person* is somehow genetic? During this time, looking for information about my ancestor Jack Nowell, the founder of Gateshead Harriers, I was very conflicted about it all. I didn't know why I felt he was important to me but I noticed that anyone I mentioned the tale to seemed to completely understand my wanting to explore the connection, without me having to explain it fully. Which I found odd. Nobody I talked to seemed to share my misgivings about the possible motive of laying claim to family pride. Or if they did, they were too polite to say.

Why should it make a difference where my genes came from? I am me, the only me there will ever be. Is a sense of belonging even a good thing, or does it simply fuel the divisions which are the true cause of our societal troubles? Communities with a strong white working-class identity were some of those who voted most affirmatively to leave Europe in the Brexit referendum in 2016. I want to blame the propaganda machines which pedalled lies about the benefits it would bring them, but I also know there are remnants of racism which the people themselves must take some responsibility for, and I want no part in that kind of culture. I know people who are really proud of their North-Eastern heritage. Geordies and Mackems are famed for their friendliness, their sense of humour, their resilience and their lovely accents. Even writing that sentence is an emotional event for me. Because I want a piece of that pride and I want to identify with those qualities of warmth and solidarity. But I can't. And I don't know if that is a conscious grown-up choice, to reject all forms of tribalism, or if it is because of family shame. The shame of what was done to me in the caravan. The shame of the idea that my mother only had sex with my dad when he raped her. I only know there is an emotional hole within me, which is my desire to belong.

I wondered about people who are adopted and have no access to their genetic family background. Nobody I have been close to is in that situation, and I can only speculate about some of the feelings and challenges it might provoke. But being me, I was scared of what I did know. Sketchy allusions to Dad's family history of schizophrenia, and he himself having epilepsy, which was still very stigmatised when I was little. The first time I saw my dad have a fit I thought he was possessed by the devil. And I was terrified that this could happen to me. This link to Jack wasn't just about a need to belong, but a need to belong to something *good*.

I was doing as Lewis had suggested—choosing to connect with an ancestor I could like. I was clutching at a straw of *goodness*. This childlike notion of *goodies* and *baddies* is striking. A framework built in my early years, which has never been properly inspected, let alone dismantled. It wasn't until I started peeling off the layers of my own prejudices and value-judgements that I began to see I was deluding myself—thinking I was free of the past. I was caught between my intellect, wanting to be rational, to feel I was the boss of my life, and my conditioned emotions about my own *badness*. It's the difference between telling myself a different story—that I wasn't built bad—and living the story.

There was little to find out about Jack himself, despite a lot of digging. Not much at all in newspaper archives or athletics archives and not even any published obituary. I did find out that Jack was the son of a hairdresser. So, my grandfather, great-grandfather and

great-great-grandfather were all hairdressers. I have always thought
of hairdressing as a healing profession. I went on a psychology
training course once where the tutor asserted that the best psycho-
therapy always takes place at the hairdresser's. That was definitely
true for my mam, who would not have missed her Friday-morning
shampoo and set for anything. During the lockdown Mandy was
worried about me giving her a haircut, but she was surprised at how
good the result was. I reassured her, 'I've got the hairdresser gene.'

I was surprised at how little of Jack's life was recorded and
wondered if it might have been because he was not a self-ag-
grandising type of person and, although he loved running, he was
not a champion himself. I wrote to the Chair of Gateshead
Harriers and he sent me a photograph of a picture hanging in the
Club's office in Gateshead Stadium. A picture of Jack with the
words 'Our Founder' underneath. I looked at the picture for a
long time; as though, if I looked long enough, he might say
something. He might speak to me; might be able to change
something. Regardless of what I thought, regardless of sense and
logic—I felt more at home in the world because of Jack. This
dead guy meant something to me. I could look at his picture and
feel a sense of calm, and strength. And a sense of belonging. I
think this is odd, and I'm embarrassed to admit it. But that's how
I feel. It's one thing knowing that we are all related to admirable,
kind and intelligent people, but it's another thing to have one right
there to look at.

My digging in newspaper archives and my vague memories of
Mam's recollections, along with stories from Jack's granddaughter,
my cousin, who is too young to have known him but has some
handed-down snippets, build up images of Jack in my mind. He
started the Harriers in 1904, and at first, they would all meet for runs
and informal races at his barber's shop. Young men and boys, sons
of the industrial revolution. They lived in cramped housing, as the

population was burgeoning despite the high mortality rates, especially in children. Running was a release from relentless hard work and something the lads could do for the sheer enjoyment of it. Despite the hardships, Jack's club grew from strength to strength until the Great War, when it was disbanded, only for Jack to get it going again as soon as the war finished, in the face of the devastating influenza pandemic which killed more people than the war itself. But Jack got Gateshead Harriers back on its feet somehow, and I wonder at the character of the man who could motivate and galvanise a group of runners in a community in a state of post-war trauma, battling through a viral pandemic, and rife with tuberculosis.

'What was he like? Do you know anything about what kind of man he was?' I ask my cousin.

'I didn't know him. But my mam said everybody liked him, and she certainly had a happy childhood, and loved her dad. She told me he was curious about everything and read a lot. He went to church like most people did, but he wasn't obsessed with religion. But he wanted to know if spirits existed, and he would set up experiments—like tying threads of cotton round door handles and to furniture at night to see if they were broken in the morning—as a way of trying to find out if there were ghosts in his house. Mam used to say that as kids they would creep out of bed and disturb his *experiments* because they thought it was hilarious.'

'What else?'

'I didn't know him. But I know he used to leave the apprentices in charge of the shop for three weeks every year and go off tramping. It wasn't anything to do with what came later, the political marches, the Jarrow Marches in the Depression. He just went to Scotland, or sometimes London, for an adventure, so he'd have something to talk about to his customers.'

'On the train?'

'No. He'd walk. He walked to London and back a few times. And all over Scotland.'

'Where in Scotland?'

'I haven't got a clue. He'd sleep in farmers' hay barns and walk thirty miles a day, or more. I don't think he got the train, or I suppose there were buses by then. But Mam said he always walked, on his own.'

'Did he have maps do you think?'

'I haven't got a clue, Julie.'

'I read about the Jarrow Marches in 1936, led by the female Labour MP they called "Red Ellen". It was desperate, they were literally starving. Did Jack have anything to do with that?'

'No, he wasn't political in that way. Anyway, I think that was a bit after his time. He just loved to go walking huge distances and come back and tell stories. That was all.'

I have a beautiful image of Jack in my mind's eye. He is waking up in a barn as sunlight streams in. All he can hear is birdsong and the bleating of lambs. He's slept well. He opens his bag and eats a breakfast of cold sausages and bread. His body feels relaxed, his mind is quiet. Nothing like when he's at home when everything's a rush in the morning, getting the coal in, lighting the fire, opening the shop to the noise of trams and the cries of the passing rag-and-bone man and the onion seller, and kids playing footy in the street before school. This morning, all Jack has to do is take in the sunshine, and the peace, and the clean air. He stands up and breathes in lungfulls. He sets off along the track, leading to who knows where. Today he's free and his body and mind are his own. I know that feeling, Jack. It's a fabulous feeling, isn't it? To be free on a sunny morning in the open air and go wherever our legs want to take us, and that might be a very long way by most people's ideas.

These stories of you tramping about the countryside, like a Geordie forerunner of Alfred Wainwright, make me wish you'd written something down. But I guess you'd never have had time for that. Working men like you were a class of doers not writers. You just got on with making things happen and didn't spare the energy to crow about them. All those stories told, while lathering up men's faces for a shave, and snipping skilfully at their hair, as you widened their horizons; they are lost now. But hearing hints of them, Jack, makes me think—I reckon you would have loved fellrunning if you'd had the chance to do it.

I'll never know you, but this illogical and sentimentalised version of you I carry inside me, Jack, it's a kind of love which has appeared from thin air. I don't know what to think about it. Because every human being is important and should be valued and nurtured, no matter who they've come from. And I don't believe in spirits either. I don't believe you are up there in some kind of heaven, willing me on and smiling when I win fell races. But there's a strength in me, a courage to not be ashamed of myself, which you have helped to nurture—from beyond your grave. To feel love for someone who was dead before I was born, as ridiculous as this may be, I'll take it. And it doesn't feel ephemeral; it feels tangible. Yes, I know these are just daft feelings and stories, Jack. But if the story of you helps me to live, then not only will I accept it, but I'll write it. I'll write the story of us, Jack, the ones who kept our heads up and kept our knees up and kept on running, and kept believing we could create our own moments of freedom.

Queer

There's a queer shaped hole in space-time
it's the exact shape of me
in every moment changing
like the waves which move the sea.

There's a story often told how
the hole is mine to choose
but I know when I make it
that's not the exact truth.

This queer shaped hole in space-time
is for me and me alone
I'm the only one who fits it
it's the only place that's home.

This is how I'm needed
and why I must be me
the other holes are taken
no hole can be left free.

10 *Survival of the Nurtured*

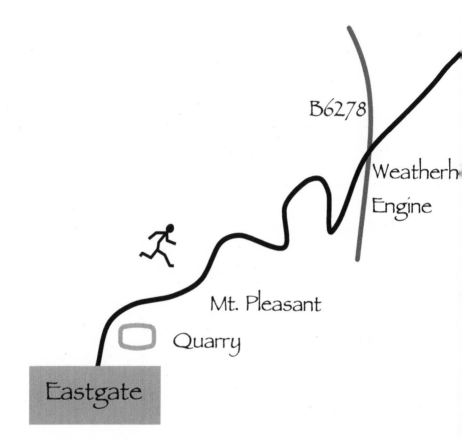

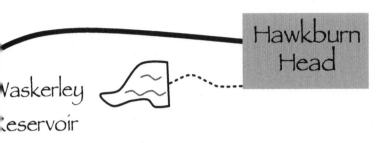

Hawkburn
Head

Waskerley
Reservoir

If the misery of the poor be caused not by
the laws of nature, but by our institutions,
great is our sin.

Charles Darwin, The Voyage of the Beagle

There was a cold wind blowing over Cullercoats beach even though it was the height of summer 1932. Two little girls were braving it out in swimming costumes, running along the sand towards the sea. It wasn't looking inviting. They squealed as they ran a few steps into the water and turned and ran back with an incoming wave. The little one lost her footing and her sister yanked her back up by the arm, laughing because she was drenched and covered in sand.

'Come on, lasses. Get ya'sels in. I'm coming in an' all. Come on. Deep breaths. Get that sea air into ya lungs. Wu'll not be havin' any sissies.'

The girls pranced forward through the waves to calmer water beyond, still just able to touch the bottom.

'Come on. Swim, our Muriel,' shouted their grandad nearby, with the water at his waist, then plunging his body in, keeping his head up to watch the bairns.

Muriel followed suit, arms outstretched and gasping with the cold, while her little sister galloped back to the water's edge.

'Eee Julie. Our Sheila and me. Wu didn't have a choice. We'd be gannin' in whether wu liked it not!' That was how my mam, Muriel, told it to me.

Then there'd be sandcastles with flags on, and sandwiches with sand in. There'd be willicks in newspaper cones; the little molluscs boiled and salted and sold with a pin to pick them out of their shells, one by one. I inherited my mother's taste for these little creatures. They had a kind of hatch over the opening of the spiral shell. To eat them, you had to pick that off and stick the pin into the soft grey flesh and then carefully wind the spiral out. The pleasure of getting one out whole, without breaking off the tail, was disproportionate to the nutritional reward. The tail was greenish, softer and more meaty tasting than the grey body but tiny, not much bigger than the pin.

Muriel and her sister Sheila were taught to swim and to eat willicks by their grandad, Jack Nowell. It never occurred to me to ask if their parents went on these outings to Cullercoats on the North Tyneside coast about ten miles from their home in Gateshead. According to Muriel, they'd go most Sundays in the summer, or was it Saturdays? She rarely mentioned those times to me, only when I complained that the sea at Amble was cold. A sort of encouragement to me to go in anyway. When she did talk about swimming at Cullercoats, it was in a vivid energised tone. There was an edge to it, like she was a bit scared of the cold, and maybe a bit scared of Jack, but at the same time thought it was brilliant. I wonder if people still eat willicks at Cullercoats or if it's all scallops and langoustines with disposable cutlery from 'seafood bars' now.

The only time I've ever been to Cullercoats myself was on 5th May 1973, shortly after my ninth birthday. I was mad about football and an avid Sunderland supporter. Dad had got three tickets for the FA Cup Final and one of them was on the back of my season ticket at Roker Park, the home ground where I never missed a game. Mam resented the fact that Dad paid for a season ticket for me, but I loved our Saturday afternoons.

Dad and me would put on our red-and-white scarves, get the bus into town and walk with the crowds to the ground, where I'd get a hot Bovril in a paper cup and it always burnt my lips. Football was fantastic. I wanted to be a footballer when I grew up. At home I would secretly put on my brother's old cast-off football strip and dance about my box room as if on the pitch, taking a penalty at Wembley. I guess it was a kind of cross-dressing. Only one of my brothers was interested in football but Dad took both of them to Wembley. He wouldn't have wanted a girl with him on Cup Final Day because then he couldn't have got drunk. I fumed at the flagrant injustice of being left behind.

For some reason, Mam's friend Vera took Mam and me to Cullercoats. When I refused to leave a shop where the match commentary was blaring from a radio, Mam dragged me out by the arm to go to the beach. And Sunderland won, one-nil, against Leeds United and I never got to see or hear it. And Dad got very drunk. The following week he paid for me to go to Roker Park to get my picture taken with the real FA Cup. And of course, that felt like no compensation at all, and I don't remember a thing about Cullercoats beach. And Mam's stories about the past and her grandad, they never concerned me anyway. I was more concerned with my quest to be unlike her than with listening to her.

Eastgate is a small village, no sign of a shop, just the main road, the bus stop with its Roman altar, the church and a few houses. The dominant feature is the main road. The many-edged sword of the internal combustion engine is something most of us have come to accept. When I'm driving along, I don't mind it of course. Then it's a great convenience. Therefore, I'm not in a position to remark on it, however much it jars my nervous system when I'm out of my vehicle and out of doors.

I'm like most people in the Western world, addicted to the car. My lifestyle is built around having access to a personal chariot, twenty-four seven. It's something I've often thought about trying to change; and although I clock up far fewer miles than I used to, I haven't manged to wean myself off it altogether yet. I've always been very sensitive to noise, but since the quiet of lockdown has been broken, I'm much less able to cope with loud sounds. Which is weak and ungrateful and hypocritical. There's a lot of tension between living in twenty-first century technological society and being an evolved flesh-and-blood creature. Not just for humans but for all of life.

Mandy is parked up a little lane, away from the main road and next to the church. I sit in the doorway of our van and drink a cup of tea while she's looking at the map.

'There's no milk left; do you think there'll be a shop in Stanhope, Jules?'

'Yes, I should think so. Mind you, I haven't been there since I used to come on cycling trips round here about forty years ago. But I reckon it's a big enough spot to get a pint of milk.'

'I have to go through there to get to the next place. Where do you think we'll stop the night?'

We confer over the map, while I dunk a couple of digestives.

'Meet me up on that little road, just past where it says 'Wetherill Engine' on the map. Maybe there'll be a spot there somewhere.'

'Okay, that's good. You've done well. Not far to go today then. See you later lovely.'

I run up the little tarmac lane, anticipating a footpath on the right in a few hundred yards. The gradient is a bit challenging and my legs are definitely tired but I'm managing to run it. I spot the finger post on the right and the gate won't open so I rally my legs to clamber over the stile. At first I keep running, short strides up through grassy fields and a lattice of drystone walls. I'm looking for a huge quarry marked on the map but there's no sign of it from below. Towards the top, I walk for a short way and as the slope eases off, a huge hole in the earth appears, surrounded by barbed wire and 'Keep Out' signs. The limestone hole is not spectacularly deep, about 30 feet, no more, but its footprint is enormous and easily big enough to fit an athletics stadium in. Above the hole are substantial but half tumbled-down stone buildings. Some sections of slate roof are semi-intact and others have their roof timbers showing through, like a threadbare patch on a rug.

The map says I need to skirt above the buildings and bear right but I notice a good path going straight ahead so I opt for that. The ground is littered with spent shotgun cartridges and I hope I'm not going to find trouble up on the moor. Coming out on a little tarmac road lined with black-and-white snow-poles, which are taller than me, I remember the Weardale Moors being famed for heavy snow. But this late afternoon is perfect, sunny and warm. I branch off the road and over the moor, taking a trod which becomes a quad bike track, before petering out altogether. Ahead is a brown featureless moor and, just in case I was getting with-drawal symptoms, there is both tussock and reedy bog to run through. I'm hoping, when I get to the top of the rise, I'll see the lie of the land. It shouldn't be far to the edge of the wood and a place going by the enticing name of Mount Pleasant.

Things are fairly serene, until my heart leaps in my chest before I even know the cause. I'm not the only runner on the moor. A hare has sprung up and is darting about like a pinball, then it disappears into the reeds as suddenly as it was triggered. How lovely! It always makes me happy to see these lop-eared athletes and I'm very much the tortoise by comparison. I can see the outline of the woodland ahead. I've come a bit too far up the moor and need to veer right, over to the farm buildings of Mount Pleasant.

When I get there, I can't see a footpath sign through the gates but everything fits on the map so I wrestle with the spring on the gate latch. I didn't do strength training for opening and closing difficult gates but, out of fear rather than duty, I'm careful to get it closed again. A tiny road leads down into the valley bottom. I'm thumbing the map like an orienteer keeping my place as I trot on and make sure this is definitely the way. It's easy downhill running but I don't want to find I've made a mistake and have to plod back up again. Past another farm, I do come to a footpath fingerpost— so ancient that it's covered in thick, pale green, hairy lichen. It points through a gate which is tied up with string, so I climb over and quickly reach the valley bottom, which is an odd place. There's an intense peace here in this little fold of earth, and also a huge modern barn. Great place for smuggling, I think to myself.

The little road I'm heading for is up a steep hill and I'm pleased to find a wending track, which irons out the gradient enough for me to keep running. But then there's a huge switchback so, true to my fellrunner's ways, I scan the steep heathery hill for a direct trod and find the sheep have created one. It's not runnable but nonetheless I'm soon up on the road. There's a few hundred yards of gentle uphill, past more tall snow-poles, and Mandy is waiting in a small pull-in. It's not a good place for the night so we decide I'll carry on a bit and we'll look at the parking at the start of the Waskerley Way cycle track another couple of miles along the road.

As Jack emerged from the sea, he pulled Muriel along with him by the hand and they caught up with Sheila, who'd started to cry and mumble resentfully, 'Too cold!'

'Come on, Sheila. We'll run up and get dressed.'

'Alright, Moo.'

Jack handed them a towel and their little blue legs ran up to the deckchairs where Muriel helped Sheila get warm and dry.

This would be the last time Jack would go in the water with them. His cough was getting worse. There would still be trips to the beach but mostly Jack would keep his shirt and jacket on, and he'd often be looking out for lots of other kids too. He would pay for a charabanc and take a tribe of children, and some of the parents, from the streets around his barber's shop. Squashing up on the wooden benches of the open-top bus, the kids would all get a 'lucky bag' paid for by Jack, with a pie and sweets and fruit. And it wouldn't take long till someone would start the singing 'The Blaydon Races' and by the time they got there at least one of them would have thrown up. It was down to Muriel and Sheila to be the best behaved.

'Set a good example, our Muriel. Shoulders back, I won't have you slouching. And I want yu in every race and the jumpin' an' all. But divunt win anything. I winnut give yu a prize, you don't need a prize. Prizes are for this lot. They've got nowt.'

They would mark out a pitch in the sand for football. Jack would organise the teams and mix them up for the rounders. Then they would mark out the running track, and then the hop-skip-jump, and out would come the skipping ropes and the quoits and finally of course, they would all be *going in*.

Muriel was eight years old in 1932, and inside her beach-blathered body, already formed and waiting, were hundreds of thousands of eggs, three of which would get to become people—my big brothers and me. I like the idea that I was present with her then. But this is only a sentimental idea; it was not me at all, only a potential me, a single cell with just over half of the genes which would finally bring me about.

My mam's cells had 23 pairs of the strings of genes known as chromosomes. Egg cells and sperm cells don't have pairs of chromosomes like most cells in our bodies, they just have one of each of the

23 chromosomes; and when they merge, the single chromosomes are paired up. As I understood it, my egg cell, with a bit more than half my final DNA inheritance, was there in Cullercoats inside Muriel. That was how we understood human genetics until recently. The scientific story was that men made their sperm continually after puberty but girls already had all their eggs inside them at birth. In the last ten years or so, it's been discovered that women may be able to make more eggs in their lifetime. My nostalgic story of my egg being already made and enjoying 1930s outings to the seaside could be a nonsense in more ways than one.

When creatures copy their DNA to make eggs, or sperm or pollen (or whatever they make, to have little ones), they have an inbuilt system to check for mistakes in the copying. My egg, as I imagined it, sitting quietly in my mother's ovary in the North Sea, would have had copies of half my mam's DNA, but the checking of those copies would not have been perfect. There are always a few mistakes. A mistake is a throw of the dice. Mistakes in DNA copying can lead to terrible inherited diseases, or they can lead to fitter, stronger, smarter offspring. Or they can be totally inconsequential. These little chance molecular happenings, along with the chance meetings—which one of millions of sperm meeting which one of thousands of eggs—these are what made the beginnings of me. And by the time I was a developing foetus, inside Muriel's womb, there were eggs developing inside me already. I came out of the womb preloaded with eggs, just like any other girl. But unlike most women who have lived through human history, I have some choices. And it was my choice that none of those cells would become a person.

Jack was getting thinner. When the charabanc arrived to collect them, and he counted all his clan back on, he turned away to cough into his hanky, to hide the blood in his spit. Like many Gateshead folk in the 1930s, Jack had tuberculosis. This little bacterial creature thrived in urban poverty. Jack had enough to eat and enough to feed his family, but it was a struggle to keep his business going and he was affected by all that was going on around him. Men who had been supporting their families with jobs in mines and shipyards and other previously thriving industries, including glassworks, mills, quarries, potteries, ironworks, brickworks and chemical works, were made jobless.

The large shipyards were slightly further down-river in Jarrow, but smaller ships were built in Gateshead where many of the supporting industries were the main employers. With the enormous slump in demand for ships and other industrial exports, there was no work and not much help. The 'dole' was difficult to access and for those who did get it, it wasn't enough. Jack's community was composed of human pawns in some far distant political game. The Great Depression began with a crisis in the financial markets in the United States. In England, the 1930s were prosperous times for many in the south, but in the industrial north unemployment was rife. Overcrowding and widespread malnutrition are the best conditions for tuberculosis to thrive in. People were living on very thin margins. More than one in ten children died before the age of five.

Jack didn't concern himself with politics. He concerned himself with his belief in fresh air and exercise. He got on the charabanc and sat at the back so he could see everyone. He knew every family and all their heartbreaks. Jack was the working man's psychotherapist. In his rented barber's shop, he got to know every story. To let him at their throats with a razor, they had to trust him. Some of his clients did think he was a bit of an odd bloke but they respected him. He thought about stuff, and he read books. Jack was a good man and he'd always help anybody if he could.

At one point, he employed a team of apprentices and ran three hairdressers' shops, but he didn't believe in owning property or accumulating wealth. He made sure his family, who lived above the shop in Melbourne Street, had enough of everything but then he gave the rest away. He would organise games in Saltwell Park for boys and girls and take great delight in handing out the prizes. He didn't wait or hope for better times, he created them. For a couple of hours here and there, on weekend afternoons on the beach, and summer evenings in the park, there was competition and camaraderie and effort and laughter and prizes. He celebrated success and he noticed who had least to eat and who never won anything for athletic ability and made sure they got something anyway. It wasn't about survival of the fittest individuals. For Jack, athletics was a way to make the whole community fitter. Jack's wife and children knew he could have saved up, could have owned a shop or a house or both. But he didn't. *Doing well for himself* was not his vision.

'It's quite busy this road, Mandy. And I'm not sure if this café will be alright about us parking up for the night. What about I carry on for the next bit and get to that marked parking on the tiny little road beyond the reservoir. Looks like about another three miles. I've come this far so I'll manage that now, and it will put us in a good position for tomorrow.'

'Yeah, okay dear, sounds fine. Do you want to take Moss?'

'Yesss. Mossy—do you want to come for a little run?'

I clip Moss's running lead round my waist and we trot off past the lovely-looking Parkhead Café, and I vow to come back one day and go in for a relaxing cuppa. Despite missing out this time, I have a lot to be happy about. Pretty much all the running which remains will be on cycleways along old railway lines which should be both easy to run on and easy to follow. It's a lovely evening and

I'm enjoying running with my faithful four-legged companion. On a good day with fresh legs, I'd cover these last miles in just over twenty minutes. I reckon it'll be half an hour or more now—but who cares?

I open the gate onto a cycleway, watched over by a sculpture of a carthorse pulling a wagon made from old pieces of rusted iron. A reminder that it wasn't always engines that did the heavy work along these old lines. The cycleway forms an arc running across the moor above the reservoir, which is off to our right. The sun is behind us, giving a low orange glow. Cyclists pass in both directions in multi-coloured lycra, speeding along in the manner of serious athletes. I don't see any other runners. Moss and I trot steadily. I have plenty of pain but I'm trying to relax, trying to tell myself neither to fight it nor ignore it. Yes pain, I hear you, but I've not got far to go. Moss is a considerate running partner and matches my pace perfectly on a slack lead. Neither of us are quick any more. Her flag-like hound's tail and her perky trot encourage me. The little road runs along the horizon slightly above us. We can't see the road itself but then we see the van moving like a mirage along the skyline.

As the charabanc drew up at Saltwell Park and everyone got off to saunter home in the calm of a summer evening, Jack took a few moments to reflect. It was a short walk to his house in Westbourne Avenue, next to the park, on one of those very still, quiet evenings when even talking in a whisper feels irreverent, as if the whole world has turned into a holy place. Jack could hear a single blackbird from all the way across the park, at the other side of the ornamental lake. He loved the fact that this park existed, right there, for everyone. The 'People's Park' had opened when Jack was only two years old and was a sign of the times; the beginning of an era when working people began to have a little time for pursuits other than the grinding need to slave away all day, every day. Jack had run in this park since he was a little lad. But his running days were over now, he knew that.

After seeing Muriel and Sheila home, and giving a quiet nod and wave to his daughter Maggie, who ushered in her exhausted daughters, Jack strolled along the edge of the park, half-wondering what the future would hold for those kids. He hoped they wouldn't go hungry and he hoped they wouldn't live through another war. And their mother was a big worry. The way she seemed to have lost her smile, and that tired look he'd noticed, and she'd been coughing a lot too. And she wouldn't say a word about herself when he managed to go round and try to talk to her, when his son-in-law Robert had gone to the horse races. He could see she was pregnant again; and she had a quiet and lifeless air about her which Jack wouldn't have thought possible when she was younger.

Maybe he was reading too much into it; she told him things were alright. When Robert had come as a lad to be Jack's apprentice, he was all keen and polite and worked hard. But as soon as he'd got a bit of money behind him, enough to rent a shop of his own, Bob Robson began to fancy himself a bit too much. When Bob had come round to Jack's house, all slicked up like a dandy to take his daughter out, Jack wasn't happy, but he couldn't stop them. He tried to warn her, but he wouldn't stand in her way. And that beautiful smile she used to have, when she'd finish playing the piano and close the lid; Jack missed that smile.

But she would never tell him anything and never say anything against Bob. There was a quiet desperation inside Jack as he watched his daughter disappear back into the house, day by day becoming a bit more diminished and shadow-like, and not knowing what he could do. Bob was always polite to Jack, too polite, and oddly formal—like a soldier being inspected by his sergeant. Neither man was at ease with the other but what could

Jack do? That's who Maggie had chosen and that was that. All Jack could do was make sure the bairns got to run outside and go to the beach and learn to swim. As long as the bairns got fresh air, Jack thought, they'd be alright.

Moss and I arrive at the van which Mandy has parked in the little car park at the crest of the last main rise before Gateshead. From here the countryside disappears down towards the coast. We are too far away to see the sea or the cities of Newcastle, Gateshead and Sunderland. But I know they are all there, just down the hill and beyond the next horizon. There's a definite sense of being somewhere different; the landscape is changing and the wild moor is about to give way to 'people-land'. It has been a long and wonderful day but yes, this car park will do nicely for tonight. Moss looks up at me to check we are stopping and then goes over to Mandy, giving her leg a gentle nose-nudge which we take to mean, 'Where's me dinner? I'm hungry.'

After stretching and changing into some clean clothes, I just lie still in the car park, on my yoga mat, and enjoy the sky, losing myself in the shifting psychedelic colours of the sunset. Imagine being a buzzard now; it would be some kind of trip to be cruising through those colours. More and more, through this pandemic, I am reminded that my attention is a precious attribute, too import-ant to squander on things that diminish rather than nourish. It's been great to have a couple of days not even thinking about the virus or interacting with any media. Some people might call it escape; I call it rebalancing.

Stretched out next to our van, I'm apprehensive. Tomorrow's run will probably end up being only a few miles longer than a marathon and all very runnable, but continuous flat running seems to aggrav-ate my bodily pain. I try to lie flat, do a body scan, and relax as much as possible. I visualise my muscles being relaxed and healthy and my spine being flexible and strong. I visualise everything feeling fine, even though that's not the sensation I'm getting. I am trying to fool my brain into thinking I'll be alright because, to some extent, we feel what we expect to feel. I'm trying to subvert the expectation machine which is my brain, but I'm not sure how to do it. Pain is familiar so I've come to expect it.

Okay, I think, it's taken 600 million years for the complexity of my nervous system to evolve from the early forms of neural nets found in jellyfish—there must be a lot of knowledge and wisdom in the body, just trust it. The Stoics' approach to life has a lot to recommend it in general, but it only really works for pain if some kind of ease can be found beyond the discomfort. Contrary to the popular saying, pain and gain are at odds. The only way I can run these days is to put every effort into being as comfortable as possible. Letting myself hurt and ignoring it, sucking it up and battling through, has been my strategy—but it is ceasing to work. There are different kinds of pain. I have spent about forty years (between about age ten and fifty) wholeheartedly committed to the Stoic method. Because to me the pain of missing out on what my running was doing for me was worse than the pain in my back and buttocks and legs. The pains that are down to the Scheuermann's disease in my spine are familiar but events in my fifties (prolapsed discs, breakage of pelvis, getting Covid) have forced me to learn a new way of living which is more about compassion than stoicism. I am learning to be aware of my pain and actively try and calm it. Learning to be kind to myself is not a way of stopping running— it's a way of being able to continue.

I find it rather disappointing that of all the basic physiological processes in our bodies, the experience of pain is the one modern Western medicine seems most nonplussed by. And now we discover there are all sorts of ways that pain is magnified when it lasts for a few months or more. The nerve endings that create the sensations proliferate. Neural pathways that transmit the signals are strengthened and the brain tunes into the signals with heightened sensitivity. When something is out of kilter and it doesn't get better, the body has to shout louder, so the *I* takes some notice. But then the *I* doesn't know what to do, because there don't seem to be any fixes; and it feels resentful, frustrated, angry and sad. Defeated, a failure. And the *I* and the body are unhappy in their marriage. Repair is needed.

I've just remembered something.

'Mandy, I need to get the books out and sign them.'

Mandy rummages under the back seat and I make a list of the people I'm hoping to meet tomorrow at Gateshead Stadium and what I want to write in their copies of my book, *Running the Red Line*, which I plan to give them. It feels a bit narcissistic to give someone a book I've written, as if they'd be interested in it—that's a pretty arrogant assumption. Never mind, it's the biggest piece of myself I can give them. And they don't have to read it—it's the thought that counts.

I pause after writing the list in my notebook and then write some stuff about how I'm feeling. After all, this is pretty special, isn't it? I'm caught between embarrassment that I ever thought anyone from Gateshead Harriers would be interested in my little run, feeling worried none of them will turn up, and feeling excited. The worries subside as I think about Jack's photograph. He'd smile wouldn't he—if he had the buzzard's eye view and could see me? I know that American Lewis believes that ancestors still have some presence as individual spirits. I don't believe that, but I still like to imagine what Jack would think about my run to Gateshead. He'd probably think I was soft, the way I am doing it. But he's not up there looking down; he's in my muscles and veins and heart, in my living tissues.

Sometimes the *I* inside me, the one I perceive as myself, seems to have very little to do with things—just an observer along for the ride. But the need to feel some personal agency is strong. I hang onto the idea of *myself* because that's how I have learnt to be. It's the current modus operandi of our species; that we are autonomous individuals, each responsible for our own survival. I wonder what it feels like to be a bee, or an ant, or a coral in a colony. Do they have *I-ness?* Perhaps the nearest thing to being part of a collective that I've experienced was being a football supporter when I was a kid. And now my red-and-white running vest is hanging over the van seat, ready for another day's running. It was Jack who designed that strip for the Harriers. They've never changed it.

Outside the van there are dozens of grouse. They all seem hyped up and happy and the cacophony of their cackles builds like a gathering crowd at a festival. The evening is a grouse gathering and their sounds are a kind of music with a rhythm and a harmony, and I lie looking at the sky and listening to the grouse music and thinking—who needs the internet when you can have this? And the air is still and sweet and infused with the remnant scents of autumn heather brought out by the warmth of the day.

Mandy gets out our little folding table to chop some veg up for dinner and I migrate into the van and put the stove on and share my ponderings.

'Mandy, do you think it's a bit spurious really—this connection with Jack and the Gateshead Harriers? I mean, I don't really think the running is in my DNA. I just happened to discover running because Linda had discovered running, because Brendan had discovered running, because his coach Stan Long had discovered running, because of Gateshead Harriers, which came about because of Jack, because running had become a thing in North-East working men's culture. It's all just a kind of accident really and nothing much to do with genetics. Do you think it's a bit weird then that I feel this sense of connection? It kind of makes sense to me, but kind of not.'

Mandy passes me the chopped-up onion for the pan and moves on to the carrot.

'It's nothing to with DNA, Jules. It's about family. Family isn't about DNA. What if you had been adopted? And anyway, you *have* been adopted by my family. And what about John? He's your family too, in effect. Family isn't about DNA; it's about who loves you and who will keep loving you, no matter what.'

'But Jack didn't love me. He died nearly thirty years before I was born.'

'Yes, but he loved Muriel.'

And so, the penny dropped. What's passed on—not a lot of it is about the DNA. Her hands were underneath my body as she set me afloat in the North Sea. Just like Jack's hands had set her to swimming in the waves. Survival of the nurtured; I get it.

Day Three

The Hard Problem

Philosophers call it *the hard problem,*
how it is that matter knows itself—
thinking on it I wonder when it was
that consciousness became a problem.

Was it during TV news seeing babies
limp and starving in heartbroken arms?
Or was it when I couldn't remember
all-important pontifications in my final exams?

Or when dull headache tiredness
switched me off—and sleep,
oh God if I only I could sleep
but the street is hard and cold.

Or when I needed to forget how
it felt when his dick ripped me open.
Cattle at the abattoir get the bullet
before the butcher.

When did consciousness become my problem?

Not after the needle went in
not after the bottle went down
not after the time when I swam
in icy silver water, saw the sunrise
melt the mist, while my skin froze
on-fire, burning itself back to life.

11 *Sweet Dreams*

The Waskerley Way

Hawkburn
Head

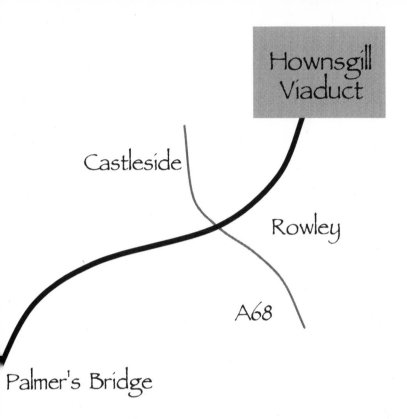

Hownsgill
Viaduct

Castleside

Rowley

A68

Palmer's Bridge

Physical self-awareness is the first step in
releasing the tyranny of the past.

Bessel van Dr Kolk, The Body Keeps The Score

T he morning is even more glorious than the evening before. Because we are facing east, the sunshine hits the van like a slick of orange luxury hurled from the horizon. The light feels more like a liquid to bathe in than a form of electromagnetic radiation which has travelled 93 million miles from our nearest star. Relishing my morning tea, I can hear Muriel's voice in my imagination; we are sitting by the window in the Bungalow Café and she's telling me, 'Yes, you know, Jack Nowell, my mam and Aunty Dinah's dad. When Aunty Dinah came over from Australia, she went to the Tartan Track and met Brendan Foster.'

While topping up my mug and enjoying the sunshine, I wonder if Brendan will come today. He's a busy important man, Sir Brendan, Olympian and President of Gateshead Harriers, the founder of the Great North Run and the reason my friend Linda inspired me to become a runner. And it must be quite tedious for him to have to entertain such unimportant people as random descendants of Jack Nowell. I wouldn't blame him for a minute if he didn't have time, and in a way, I can't see why he would come. But then again, we are in a post-lockdown phase and maybe, like the rest of us, he hasn't been getting out much, so this quirky reason for a trip to the stadium might just tempt him. I'm trying to be realistic and not get my hopes up. He really must have more important things to do.

Tea, porridge, stretching on the car park yoga mat under a blazing orange sunrise in my dirty, sweaty red-and-white vest. I have more time to relax today, before the off. It should be the easiest running day by far, only about 28 miles, maybe less, and all much less hilly and on better paths than the previous days. I am excited and curious as to what the day will bring, and also nervous in case the pain of flatter running just grinds me to a halt. I'm still not exactly sure of my own motives, but I try not to tangle myself up in analysis. I'd better get going now. I need to be nearing Gateshead by lunchtime and it's a good idea to leave a bit of time in hand for stretching breaks if needed. I walk the few yards back to where I left off yesterday, onto the well-made cycle-track which will lead me ever eastwards, and I slowly ease myself into a run.

Meanwhile, about 20 miles down the Tyne Valley, my friend Jenny Power is in her front garden oiling her bike chain when her next-door neighbour happens to come out.

'Off far today, Jenny?'

'I'm just riding out to meet my friend who's running from Keswick to Gateshead Stadium. I'll guide her in on the bike, so she doesn't get lost through the city.'

'Oh, that woman who's the great-granddaughter of the Gateshead Harriers' founder. The champion fellrunner. Great story that, isn't it? Great thing to do.'

'Yes, but how did you know?'

'Oh, just heard about it on the radio five minutes ago.'

Which seems surprising, since we didn't know anyone had cotacted the radio. It isn't that kind of thing. It's not a media thing; it's personal. But Jenny and her neighbour are quite excited, as she prepares to set off pedalling to meet me somewhere along the old railway line of the Waskerley Way. I just have to keep running and keep following the blue-and-white cycleway signs pointing towards Newcastle until I meet her.

For a few miles I don't meet anyone at all along the engine-wide finely graded track, which relinquished its redundant rails in 1985. This railway was part of the pioneering technology which powered the industrial revolution and has now changed into a recreational track for cyclists, runners and walkers. This line mostly supported a goods service, transporting coal and lime from the Weardale moors to the Tyne Valley and South Shields. It was opened in 1845 by the Stockton and Darlington Railway, the same company which, twenty years earlier, had opened the first passenger steam train service in the world.

The railway revolution was catalysed by the genius of a working-class lad from Wylam called George Stephenson, who was born close to where Jenny's bike is waiting in her garden. Legend has it that, when deciding on the gauge of the railways on which to run the steam engines, George went to the Roman fort of Housesteads on Hadrian's Wall to measure the ruts in the stones of the east gate, made by the Roman chariots. It's the 'Just So Story' of how the railways got their gauge. Four feet eight and a half inches became standard width for railway tracks throughout the world. The path under my feet has a past. A boy from the Tyne Valley who could not read until he was eighteen and who did not have formal education became the 'Father of the Railways'. He drew on all the past ingenuity and knowhow available, including the remnants of a local Roman fort, and as a result, for better and worse, railways remapped the world. Running along the nicely manicured present-day Waskerley Way, I realise how tightly everything is knit, and suddenly our planet seems outrageously small and all of human history very short. When history becomes tangible, it's no longer just in the past.

There are fields to my left and a plantation of pines on my right and I'm looking out for a short cut to miss out a long slow bend in the track, but I don't find it. What I *am* finding are fleeting moments of deep connection and legitimacy, as if the very idea of questioning my little part in the ecosystem is impossible. Perhaps it's the railway line, the sense of everything being joined up. Jenny has probably set off from Wylam by now. I wonder how long it will be before we meet. She cycled the route a couple of weeks ago and sent me a series of pictures to help me navigate through the built-up areas, in case something goes wrong, like if she gets a puncture, and we miss each other. I have no doubt she'll be there, though. I'll just keep following the line.

Bodies change through experience. By the age of twenty-one, after four years of running, I was pretty good, even though I didn't know anything whatsoever about how to train. I came in the top twenty in the British Students' Cross-Country Championships, and I'd run an hour and twenty-six minutes for a half marathon. At the time I didn't realise this was quite respectable for someone who had not been into sport at school, and although I loved the races while they were happening, I didn't make much of the results and just looked forward to my next run.

Running changed my bodily experience of living; from being weak and powerless running made me feel strong and free. Until the year after I graduated, when I found myself half-awake in the intensive care unit of York Hospital. I spent a week of feverish days and nights there, with very little consciousness. I have hardly any memory of it. Just one song on a Walkman tape which I hung onto. And maybe it wasn't on a tape—even though I seem to remember the box cover, maybe it was in my head. Annie Lennox was in the hospital with me, singing 'Sweet Dreams'. It was my lullaby. I can't remember the room or if there was natural light but I had a sense of day and night because the fever was worse at night. It was a brain-busting, bone-melting fever of over 41 degrees, and I was scared of it as night approached.

'Sweet Dreams' interrupted my nightmares and calmed me. It's the kind of song lyric that asks more questions than it answers, and I could hear something in Annie Lennox's voice which wasn't only words. It was strength and resilience and love-of-life, even when things are desperate. If I play that song now, I think I can cope with anything. Because my body knows when it hears that song that it can survive. Even at times when I feel like my life is over—I hear a few bars of Annie Lennox and my instinct is to live. All living beings need courage to carry on; daily life is an act of faith. I think every biological being has ways of connecting up what's good and safe and life-giving. Or else we wouldn't be here at all. None of us would have survived. And a few days after the initial blur of being really ill I was transferred to my own room. The nurses would come in, all masked and gowned, and I could feel I was getting stronger. One morning I woke up flooded by an overwhelming sense of relief because I'd slept through the night without the terrible pain of the fever, and I thought, 'Maybe I'm not gonna die, I'm not gonna die after all!' Then, five minutes later, a male nurse came in and took my temperature, pulse and blood pressure and mumbled through the mask, 'We've found out what you've got. It's pretty nasty.'

And then he took off his gloves, washed his hands methodically and left.

'Oh shit—maybe I *am* gonna die then.' I was only twenty-one. But I felt like I had lived long already, so maybe this was really it.

A couple of weeks earlier I had been in India. It was my first trip abroad by aeroplane and I had gone alone for a few months to both India and Nepal to explore the mountains. As Annie Lennox sang, I had travelled the world; isn't everybody looking for something.

I had run away from an abusive marriage. In the last year of my degree, I had followed our family tradition and married young, to a cruel psychopath. I was in love with him. He came to visit me in hospital with his girlfriend, to snog her in my hospital room. He was rude to the staff and acted like my illness was an entertaining curiosity, as if he thought 'Oh, what fun, to be the first ever patient in York Hospital to be diagnosed with typhoid. Kudos.' But—Annie Lennox never deserted me. She seemed to know all about my situation when she sang about 'some of them' wanting to use and abuse you.

I left hospital weighing under six stone (38kg) and, although I didn't appreciate it at the time, my psyche and my genetics were changed forever. I had effectively been through a starvation experience and the whole of my metabolism was thereafter geared towards the conservation of energy. Bodies learn. Within a few months, I was over nine stone (57kg), a stone heavier than my previous usual weight. It wasn't just gluttony. My system had been retuned and my genes were being expressed in different ways.

DNA molecules are basically long strings of code, very much like this sentence, except they are much longer, and all the words have only three letters. Each three-letter code determines which one of a selection of molecular building blocks will be added to a protein to make up the structural and functional elements of our bodies. That's why DNA is called a 'blueprint', like an architectural plan. Early in the twenty-first century, when the entire DNA of a human was read (or *sequenced*) for the first time, geneticists got a shock. They had anticipated finding upwards of 100,000 specific genes, DNA sequences which each translated into the code for a specific protein. But they found only 20,000. The rest of the DNA didn't contain code that could be translated to building proteins; it just seemed to be a nonsense of jumbled-up letters. In the usual style of arrogant know-it-all science, this quickly became known as 'junk DNA'. If we don't understand what it's doing, it can't be important.

Geneticists haven't yet figured out exactly what the 'junk DNA' is doing, but it seems to have a lot to do with the switching on and off of the genes themselves. It's like the conductor of an orchestra. We can carry certain genes within us which can remain unexpressed for most of our lives, like a percussion instrument which is only played for a few seconds in a whole symphony. The junk DNA is the maker of all the little messages, called messenger RNAs, which stick to the genes, telling them when to work and when to rest. The orchestration is so complicated that more of our DNA is needed to control the genes properly than to code for the genes themselves.

There are all sorts of ways that parents pass on signals which help their bodies survive; even some of the little messenger molecules, the RNAs, can get passed on. If our bodies are symphonies, it's as if the musical score has come with the previous conductor's pencil notes in the margins. Even though I'd just finished a genetics degree I didn't know any of this—because it was only 1986 and it would take another twenty years before anyone knew it. Even now, little is known about how inherited molecules other than DNA affect our biology. The very idea that all our biological inheritance is not just through DNA is a revolution in genetics.

One of the most profound experiences a creature can have, in terms of altering the orchestration of its genes, is starvation. The willingness of a body to burn up its energy is key to endurance running. I know from my own experience that the typhoid changed my metabolism; but science is not based on a sample of one, and how exactly this all works is still unknown. What was horribly real was the weakness and lethargy I was struggling with. I worried about whether I would run again. And thus far running had been my salvation. Surely, even fortified by her advice to keep my head up and move on, I wouldn't be able to survive on Annie Lennox alone.

Still chugging along on the Waskerley Way, I'm getting hot already; and, although my back and pelvis hurt, I'm running fine and enjoying being on my own. I have plenty of time today, even if I have to stop for a rest. My mind keeps chuntering on, trying to articulate thoughts. To my logical brain, which likes one thing to obviously follow from another in a sequence of time and causality, the memories which arise seem random. But there are layers within us, instincts and hunches which don't quite make sense in a linear way. When things don't make sense, running helps. Don't think about something, go for a run and then suddenly, halfway round, everything drops into place. How to sort out a chapter that's not working, how to approach a troublesome person, how to live my life more in tune with myself. The answers miraculously arrive. Something is happening inside my body when I run that isn't just to do with blood and muscle. An unconscious capability is being tapped into—a way of *getting* the world, which depends more on practice than theory.

Every now and then, there's a road crossing at some land-that-time-forgot kind of place. These little villages in County Durham, where miners and railway workers lived, feel a little ghostly. People still live here but I wonder what sustains these communites; where is the glue of common experience and purpose, now that everyone has to travel to disparate work? Every time I leave the track to cross a tarmacked road, my rhythm is broken. Standing by a pedestrian crossing next to a boarded-up pub and waiting for the lights to go red, there is disconnection—fracture. Earlier, when I was alone, I felt connected, but now, wary of strangers, I'm on guard.

I sprint over the road and I'm looking for the blue-and-white cycleway signs to get me back on track. I pass the occasional person on a bike and family with children and pushchairs and feel quite self-conscious in my Gateshead Harriers' vest. Do I deserve to be wearing it? I'm not even a member of the club. I come from somewhere else—normally I wear a different colour shirt. The transgressive emotion I so often get is welling up in my stomach. Don't belong, don't fit-in. I don't like this misfit feeling, and I wonder why it is there. All I am doing is running. An aging bent woman in a club vest, running—is that weird?

Why do I so easily feel like an outsider? I want to know where my niche is in the ecosystem. Sometimes I have felt a sense of belonging but that has been rare. Singing 'Haway the Lads' as a kid with my dad in the stands at Roker Park, cheering on my red-and-white-shirted heroes. And when I was part of a team in my Cumbrian running club in which, for a while, I felt at home. In relays where we competed together and gave our all for the team, or just shared running together and our love of the fells. But the older and slower I get, and the less willing I am to tolerate the laddish behaviour which seems to have infected the running club, the more I feel isolated and frozen out of a group I once thought were my tribe.

Things change, it's only natural. Everyone's life has moved on. I still have good friends I shared those team efforts with, but—more and more—I run on my own these days. And while I love the freedom of that, sometimes I miss the feeling of being in a team. Races were always good get-togethers, but since breaking my pelvis I haven't raced much and now Covid has broken us even further apart. As well as the shifts in the culture of fellrunning in Keswick, and the shift in my own tolerance of toxic masculinity, the pandemic is prising open the fracture lines even wider. The virus seems to be dissolving some of the glue which holds us together; and when this is all over, I don't know what the repair process will be like. Will I run in the yellow and green of Keswick or the red and white of Gateshead or neither and does it matter? A vest is just a symbol and it doesn't mean anything if the underlying connection is not really there.

Back on the old railway, I'm now surrounded by tall trees and grateful for their shade. Running in the full sun today would be tough going. Now I'm away from habitation again, I'm on my own and the seclusion is a welcome protection against embarrassment. My mam always said I was 'painfully shy' but I don't think it really was shyness—more a deeply conditioned sense of 'stranger-danger'. And in my world everyone felt like a stranger, even the people I lived with. The trees shading the old railway are the nearest beings to my heart right now. I try and focus on the trees and feel their presence. When people cannot hold my heart, other beings can, especially trees, whose aged arms feel strong and reliable. At this moment I feel lonelier than ever and I don't fight the feeling. But I keep looking to the trees for companionship.

I'm often curious about the experience of other species. How do they sense themselves and the world? What do they know? What would it be like to be tree or bird, insect or worm? I have to accept the not-knowing, the great mystery, because I only really have me. It's hard enough to understand the inner experience of my fellow humans. This loneliness—it's not just a mood or feeling. It's beginning to occur to me that loneliness is not my failure but is just a property of nature. I can share things, but I can never know exactly what another's experience is like. Things I call green, Mandy sometimes calls blue, which isn't just semantics. Our perceptions are different, no matter how much I love her and how closely we are connected. The trees are still in leaf today, mostly green, with some yellows beginning to come through. They are preparing for the great autumnal letting go. The path is built on what I presume is an old railway embankment, and the tree bottoms are well below me as I run past the elegant trunks and branches of hundreds of birches. Some kind of paradox is flipping about inside me. Only through accepting my aloneness, my individuality, will I find the connection I seem to need. Loneliness and aloneness are not the same thing. One is a painful clinging on; the other is the relief of letting go.

Ahead of me is what looks like a silver tunnel but as I get closer I see it's the curved metal suicide railings on the Hownsgill Viaduct. This fifteen-span, three-million-brick edifice, built a couple of decades before my great-grandfather Jack was born, is a sight to behold. I am inside what feels like a topless tube looking out above the tree canopy. I'm not sure if I've ever looked down on a big old oak before. The need to stop and peer is too much and, despite the wires of the enclosing safety fence, the view from the middle of the viaduct makes me even more envious of birds and their eye-views. Looking down onto this tapestry of leaves and branches, it's fantastic. But the trees have not been enough for some poor folk. It's saddening to know that the fence was built as a response to a spate of suicides, which for the first half of 2011 averaged one every two weeks. I wonder why it was that despair reached its zenith so recently.

The town of Consett nearby has been through worse times. When the steelworks closed in 1980, unemployment hit 36 per cent. Once the steel capital of the world, until it was usurped by Sheffield, Consett steelworks was a vital part of the 'great northern powerhouse'. Growing up in the North-East in the 1970s and '80s, I imbibed the narrative of decline; the idea that this was a no-hope, cultureless kind of place. But the late twentieth century decline was just a snapshot—this region had earlier been a hothouse fuelling the world's ecomony through its ships and glass and steel and steam engines and railways.

A heavy weight of heritage is present in this place, which powered the aristocratic project of Empire. The North-East gave the knowhow and the labour, the blood and the sweat and the brains, but reaped little of the reward. All that coal and rock heaved out of the earth and dragged along this line I am running along now—it wasn't for the health of the miners or the health of the planet. You could say that global warming was pioneered here. When a friend of mine drove past Consett in the 1970s he said the black fumes and orange flames above the steelworks were 'like Modor'. But the community did not want it to close. Our creativity and bigger visions have been stifled by the want of a basic income. We need to eat. And maybe the desperation of long-term decline took a few decades to bite hardest because the world has moved on. In the new millennium the effective slavery of the working classes in England during the previous two hundred years is often overlooked, as if class is an irrelevant concept now. Depression and suicidality do not result from faulty genes but from the complexities of the social structures we are caught up in. If we are not in a class war any more, is that because we have lost the fight? History has robbed certain demographics of their hope. I set off again and leave the canopy view and the viaduct behind. I am running faster now. Anger always makes me run faster.

Surely the worst thing we ever invented was our class system— all the wealth and benefit to the bosses that came on the backs of the workers. It's not so much that a few people got very rich and a lot of people got very poor, it's what it did to our *souls*. The story handed down and believed in. That we, the great unwashed working class of the North-East, were fit for little other than slaving with our bodies for other people's profit. Bollocks to it!

For me the worst of it is how taken in and steered by the storytelling of my bourgeois betters I am. Don't get me wrong— I'd rather have my fingernails pulled out by the roots than vote Tory, but scratch a little deeper than the colour of my vote and you'll find an almost desperate devotion to the myth of meritocracy. I've always wanted to climb the ladder, to be respectable.

Now the sun is high in the sky and the day is getting hot. I have no more layers to take off, on the outside, but inside the layers are unpeeling. This is difficult—but good. Understanding more of how I got to be where and how and who I am. And running? Is that just another way of buying into deluded value judgements about *bettering myself*? Good question, but no. It isn't just that. It's so much more than that.

Not very long after the viaduct, I settle back into a more relaxed pace; and gazing ahead, I see Jenny in a high-vis vest approaching on her metal steed. We both stop. Should we hug? How unnatural it is not to hug Jenny. But better not with the virus still about. I haven't seen my friend for months and I can't presume, even though we are outside.

'How was the ride Jenny?'

'Oh great. What a morning! Fabulous. Great to see you. How are you feeling? Do you need a drink or anything? Can't believe how warm it is already.'

'Yeah, drink of water. Lovely. Thanks.'

'Anything to eat?'

'No, I'm okay. Had porridge before I left. Amazing sunrise, just amazing.'

'Let's keep going then. You tell me if you need anything. Great to see you—just great.'

After my bout of typhoid in 1986, life was messy and I needed to sort myself out. I moved away from my troubles with the horrific husband in York to do a PhD in evolutionary genetics at Bath

University, and to fulfil my desire to be a proper scientist. In the hardest of times, the impulse to just run, to enact escape, felt like the most meaningful thing I could do. But it was difficult to get running again after the typhoid. One weekend, in Bath, there was a low-key student race and, on a whim, I joined in. Since nobody knew me, I wouldn't feel so embarrassed about being slow. As we lined up on the playing field in lashing rain, I felt the spark of energy which running always brought.

After a couple of miles I felt like I'd woken up from a year-long bad dream. I suddenly found my legs, my lungs, my heart, myself. I felt like I had broken back into the current of life, running in a stream of energy, after being stranded in some dark and stagnant eddy. I was racing, flying downhill with the brakes fully off. Huge raindrops bounced off the road while a grumbled warning of thunder rumbled in from distant hills. No lightning yet, but my nerves and muscles were sparking at full throttle as I chased down the steep road from Bath University up on the hilltop towards the bourgeois little city nestled in the valley. Running, flying, absorbing and releasing elemental forces. Until my right foot hit an uneven kerb and bang—it all stopped with an undignified clatter. I got myself upright and could hardly bear to put any weight on my ankle. Wincing and crying, I hopped and stumbled back up the hill and took a short cut over the field to the medical centre. In the coming days my ankle was enormous and blue. I needed crutches to get about and couldn't sleep for the pain. And again, it was months before I could run.

A week after rupturing my ankle ligaments, I was propped up at my lab bench, distracted and failing to get my work to progress. I went back to my lodgings and went to bed. I stopped getting up in the mornings, and soon it was all I could do to drag myself to the University later in the day; and when I was there, I couldn't concentrate, and would fall asleep or just cry. What had happened—where had I gone?

I had the chance to do a fantastic project, to extract and sequence the DNA of a very special little bug which lived at high temperatures and was different to any other type of life. One thing all biologists are curious about is how life got started in the first place. In the 1980s the family tree of life was divided into two domains, which together contained five kingdoms: bacteria, protozoa, fungi, animals and plants. Because all living things have common features, such as the presence of molecules like DNA, it seems reasonable to assume that all life on Earth has a single common ancestor. From this ancestor, back in the days of the 'primordial soup', there eventually emerged more complex creatures which led to the myriad of life forms belonging to the five kingdoms. Something must have led to those, preceded them, given rise to them. At some point there must have been a common ancestor; and if we could find something like that ancestor still living, then we could maybe find out about the very beginnings of life. Biologists called this hypothetical creature LUCA—the last universal common ancestor.

I nicknamed my little bug 'Archie' because it was from a group of bugs then called Archaebacteria. There were reasons to think that Archie could really be LUCA, since Archie didn't fit into any of the five kingdoms but had molecular features in common with creatures from all of them. Right from the times of peering into pools on Amble beach, I had been fascinated by the question of how the plethora of creatures I found there came to be the way they were. If we knew Archie's DNA code and compared it to that of other creatures, we should know a lot about how life got going. This project was as exciting as having a living dodo, unicorn and sabretooth tiger all parading around my lab asking to be examined. Why was I not getting into work at 7am every day and staying until midnight?

It was the lead that filled my veins. The same feeling I'd known since primary school. I felt as if somebody had pulled my plug and let all my water out, then filled me up again with lead. I didn't know what was wrong. I just felt *I* was wrong. I could not possibly step into this world of being a true scientist. I had always known it was all a pretence. My mother's explanation that I had been a mistake rang true. Isolated from anyone I knew, it became a fight to get up, to eat, to speak; even the most basic signs of life were too much to muster. My comfort was in bottles of strong cheap wine, not because I enjoyed drinking, but just because it made things less painful. I gave up the PhD, went back to York and got a job in a warehouse, packing plants for garden centres. I did not feel happier, but I did feel more at home, on the production line.

Ours

Ours was halfway down the wide street, on the edge of the council estate.

Ours was the one with the roses in the little front garden from which my mam picked up
empty crisp packets and cans.

Ours didn't have dandelions like the other houses, the flowers my friends threw in my face,
to make me wet the bed.

Ours was where I couldn't get out to play, so I climbed through the first-floor window.

Ours was where I stood on the slim concrete sill over the front door watching my mates kick
the one ball into anything that was breakable.

If you go there now, you'll see that ours is the place where I couldn't get down.
You'll see me, still there, stuck to the wall, in my nighty, in the evening sun.

12 *Just Keep Going*

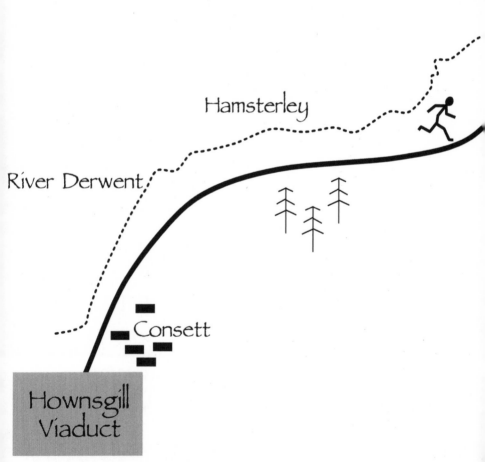

Rowland's Gill

Hamsterley

River Derwent

Consett

Hownsgill
Viaduct

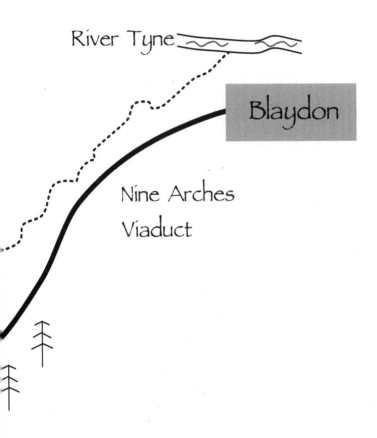

River Tyne

Blaydon

Nine Arches
Viaduct

The opposite of addiction is not sobriety.
It is human connection.

Johann Hari

'Our Father, witch art in heaven…'

Sitting behind my primary school desk, head bowed and hands folded together, I didn't understand this ritual. What bothered me most was the idea of 'witch-art in heaven'. I formed a mental picture of evil black crones parking their broomsticks somewhere on a cloud, and painting artworks to hang in heaven. It was disturbing. Then the bell would go, and I would wrestle my chair onto the desk, chair legs heavenward, and I'd hang back at the coat rack to avoid the rush.

I was a small girl, whose body weighed a hundred tons, dragging herself up the school drive at the end of lessons. The school was at the bottom of a concrete drive with big iron gates at the top. It wasn't a long or steep slope but that small girl was always last through the gates. On the afternoons when she felt very heavy like this it also struck her how quiet everything was. It was almost like she had lost her hearing. She walked home alone in silence, as if she and the world had nothing to say to each other. She was locked inside an iron skin.

Depression isn't an illness; it's an excruciatingly painful signal that something is wrong which needs attention. The frozen feeling of being locked inside a lonely prison was familiar to me, but I had always thought I would escape, and that passing exams would transport me to some kind of freedom. At York I had found some friends and I'd found running, but my undergraduate degree was only a staging post.

Arriving in a posh southern university as a PhD student, I was like a refugee who had clung to the life-raft of education and reached a solid shore, only to find myself an outsider with no resources and little understanding of the language or culture. Like many people who have been on a journey of escape, reaching what could be seen as some kind of dream destination is the time when things fall apart badly. It's the time when the monster black dogs from under the bed come out and hunt you down. Because up to that point there has been a purpose, the journey to freedom and safety and a better life. Purpose is everything. In the words of the doctor and Auschwitz survivor Viktor Frankl, 'He who has a *why* can bear any *how*'.

Bath University, with its huge modern concourse surrounded by beige-coloured blocky buildings all bunched together like a three-dimensional puzzle, felt like a spaceship—and I felt like an alien. Perhaps if my heart hadn't been unmoored by the bad husband, I would have had the courage to integrate, and by now I'd be some well-known professor whose work was part of the canon of biological knowledge, a little piece in the jigsaw whose edge pieces had been put together by Mr Darwin.

I have regrets. Don't we all have regrets? I've learned not to patronise my regrets by trying to look on the bright side. I reckon it's better to look the regrets right in the eye and ask them what they have to teach me, so I don't end up making all the chapters of my life into Groundhog Days in different settings. When I went back to York, after deserting my PhD, I had two important things. I had my best friend, John (of the birthday cake and bovine near-miss), and I had the run along the River Ouse, out of town and past the delicious smell of chocolate factories to the meadows beyond. And I did the same run almost every day for months, and if some days it was the only thing I did, then that was okay because on that run there was no leaden depression in my veins, no sick anxiety in my guts. There was just running and somehow running was enough.

Family studies involving identical and non-identical twins are commonly cited as evidence that the emotional experiences which we collectively add together and call depression can be partly caused by genetics. But what we inherit is not a cause of these emotions, it is a susceptibility to them. Some plants in my garden are susceptible to frost but they are fine unless the temperature is very cold. Likewise, we are fine when the conditions we live in meet our needs. Like any living creature, we have requirements for health; and for most humans these seem to include love and attention, connection and meaning, and a sense of purpose. There may be a complicated mix of genes which, if they get expressed in certain ways, make us a bit more vulnerable to the consequences of unmet needs. But there are no genes for depression. And there are circumstances where even unsusceptible people will get very low. When I was a doctor, I found it interesting how clusters of people living in a certain area, or working for a certain employer, seemed to say they were depressed. If the frost is hard enough, it can kill almost anything.

At Lydgetts Junction, Jenny and I pass an old iron-coloured railway truck whose two blobby buffer arms at the front make me think of the Daleks on *Dr Who* that used to terrify me into hiding behind the sofa as a child. The industrial relic feels almost out of place now, amongst the green surroundings. We immediately make a quick turn and emerge onto an A road near a roundabout beside Morrison's supermarket in Consett.

'We have to cross this side road now, Jules, but stay on the left of the main road. Righto, it's clear now, run—straight across.'

We go along a main road, past a Tesco and a Costa and a McDonald's, with their huge logos like triumphant heraldic badges displaying their allegiance to global capitalism. For a while I run on a grass verge to ease my legs after the hard ground of urban sprawl. We turn between stone gate posts into a park, taking twists and turns, passing dogs and their walkers, children and their parents, bikes and their riders. I feel safe running alongside Jenny in her high-vis vest on her bike, equipped with an excellent bell which she inherited from her dear brother.

'It was one of Edward's favourite things, this bell,' she tells me, remembering him fondly. Jenny also has a speedometer on the bike.

'Your pace is the same, just over 7 miles an hour. It's been virtually the same all the time I've been with you, you're doing well. Do you need a drink or anything?'

'Yes, thanks, I'll have water. Never expected it to be this hot by a long way.'

During a series of streets and road crossings, there are occasional blue-and-white cycleway signs encouraging me on. Gateshead— only 14.5 miles. Not far at all, only a little further than a Great North Run. But I am so glad to have Jenny. Getting past Consett didn't look that bad on the map, but in practice it would have been a nightmare without her. A bit further on, the line of the old railway resumes its incarnation as the Derwent Walk Cycleway. Through some bollards and back onto a tree-lined track and our ears can relax again, away from the traffic. The running is pleasant, along the tarmac-free line sheltered by big trees.

'It's like this all the way now, for another 7 miles, to Rowland's Gill. I'll message Mandy and let her know how we are doing. Great progress, Jules. Really good. Just keep going, I'll catch up.'

I'm on my own for a few moments with the sounds of birds and my own feet, until Jenny's wheels join me again. It's a lovely run along the Derwent Way, surrounded by oaks, and alders, hawthorns and holly. I didn't expect this wildlife haven, not here. Jenny and I chat easily but there are also easy silences, which neither of us feel inclined to fill. She doesn't overdo the chat, or the encouragement, or anything else for that matter. She is considered and relaxed and it just feels good to have her cycling along with me. I don't feel tired, the going is easy, but my back aches quite a lot. I start thinking I might have to stop for a few minutes and stretch. It might be a good idea. Don't want anything to stop me making it to the end now, after running all this way.

In Mrs Colclough's sixth-form biology class, we learnt our lessons through storytelling. Because she always told us the context and the characters involved, we understood each chapter was not a truth set in stone but a stage in the plot. Knowledge changes, develops and expands. In terms of the story of my little bacteria Archie, the tale has taken some dramatic turns in the last three decades, while I have been otherwise occupied. Archie and relations, classed as bacteria when I knew them, are now in a domain of their own, the Archaea, within the creature classification system. To put this promotion in context, there are only three domains in the family of biological life: prokaryotes (mainly bacteria), Archaea (Archie and his relations), and eukaryotes (everything else, from amoebae to worms to us).

Archaea were around first, before bacteria and before the more complicated life forms developed. But it all gets very murky in the deep and distant past because this story of life, where creatures inherit a DNA blueprint from their parents, gets less and less reliable, the smaller the critters are. Because microbes don't just give their DNA to their offspring but they also give it to each other, in an unscrupulous orgy know as 'horizontal gene transfer'. Strange little things, like viruses, and pieces of genetic material called transposons, which are not independent life forms, but just part beings, cut and paste themselves into the cells of other living things, carrying DNA from one host to another, even across different species.

DNA is not only inherited; it's kind of picked up along the way too, and as much as 8 per cent of human DNA is likely to be from viruses, which have wheedled their way into our chromosomes over millennia and then get copied and passed on as if they were part of us. And of course, they *are* part of us, sometimes helping our cells to function and being a source of some of the spontaneous variety which natural selection can then pare down to the forms which suit the environment. All this 'family tree of life forms' business is far more complicated than I ever imagined when I was failing to stand up at my PhD lab bench. Life, not just humanity but all of life, really is more of a tapestry than a tree.

Looking for a place to fit into the ecology of my world, I went from PhD student to plant-packer to science teacher to outdoor education instructor to medical doctor; always trying to look ahead to the future—because the past was over and done with and couldn't be altered and was best not dwelt upon. That was my outlook. And I don't think I made a bad job of any of it. I always worked consciously and tried to be creative and caring, especially as a medic.

My only trouble as a doctor was the philosophy of mechanistic reductionism, viewing people as the sum of their body parts, which casts its ugly shadow over what is an essentially humanitarian pursuit. Nobody ever had trouble with my competency or capacity to be effective, as either plant-packer or teacher or medic, but they did have trouble with my habit of questioning. Questioning a system which dehumanised and poisoned in the name of kudos and profit. Fitting in—it's always been my problem. Maybe some virus will come along one day and infect me with a dose of pragmatism.

I left my first job in general practice because of a cover-up, which I was—accidentally—party to exposing. I left my second job because I wasn't posh enough or conventional enough for my colleagues. After that I managed to keep my head under the parapet but it always felt like a contortionist's act. It was never the hours or the workload or the hard sad business of medicine that pushed me out. It was the stress of practising in a way which contravened something fundamental about me. It was the requirement to have a closed mind, attending to parts not wholes, employing flimsy fixes over possibilities for actual healing. Yet even so, I often found the work good and rewarding on the inside of a consultation. I didn't find it hard to connect with people who were suffering; but forging relationships with other doctors was a desperate strain. I wondered why and how they'd seemingly got so sure of themselves. It almost felt like medics were becoming a different breed of organism to patients. I understood why so many people 'don't like doctors'. I was very disconnected from most of my colleagues, and unconvinced by the prevailing culture within medicine. Over the years, a tension built up within me which became too painful to live with.

So, if I cannot be woven into life's tapestry through meaningful work, and I have hardly any living family or sense of belonging to a particular place, and don't even feel at home in my running club any more, where will I find my tribe? The writer Johann Hari describes our generation as the first in human history to dismantle our tribes. In part, this is a good thing if it means less prejudice and violence. But on a very personal level it leaves us feeling stranded, and Hari cites this lack of 'being woven in' as one the major causes of rising rates of anxiety and depression. It's hard to find meaning in solitary pursuits. Am I just the end dot in a branch line—an evolutionary end of the tracks?

I could drown myself in existential angst but for the fact that when I run, the feeling of air down the back of my throat quenches my thirst just as it did in the playground and it comes down to this—I run therefore I am. Something here goes far back in deep-time. You could argue about whether our little buggy ancestors were conscious or not, but in their molecules and, in their beha-viour, for four-and-a-half-billion years they have asserted the principle that life has intrinsic value. The glorious complexity of biology which pulses within me is 8 per cent virus and 2 per cent Neanderthal but 100 per cent alive. Whether I'm tired or fresh, every time I run it's not just that I am this creative life energy, but I also *know* I am. This whole tribe thing, I can see why we've needed it and how it evolved. But the dichotomy of wanting to be a free individual with agency and yet a part of something more meaningful than just me—the joy of living pulsing biology—makes all that turmoil seem like nothing but words. When I run, I understand that I *am* pure biology, a free animal who is related to every other living being and all that's gone before. Do I need the smallness of a tribe when I can have the hugeness of life itself?

I've still got about 10 miles to go to Gateshead. At one time I thought anything more than that was a long run but fellrunning often demands being out for several hours so I've got used to keeping going; and if not for the pain that gnaws away in my pelvis, it would take a lot more than another 10 miles for me to feel fatigue.

There used to be a dogma in exercise physiology—that certain people are good at long distances because they are born with a lot of *slow twitch* muscle fibres, whereas sprinters have a good endow-ment of *fast twitch* muscle cells. While we can train our muscle fibres, we cannot alter the slow/fast twitch ratio, which is innate, determ-ined by the genes we inherit. But like most dogma, this turns out to be an oversimplification. Until we exercise, a lot of the muscle fibres sit on the fence and are *indeterminate*; they can develop into either endurance muscle or sprinting muscle. Sprinting or lifting weights will provoke those cells into being fast twitchers, which are very powerful but tire quickly. But if you run steadily for hours on end, the on-the-fence fibres will develop in ways that favour endurance. And if you do nothing, the muscles gradually lose their adaptations for either power or endurance.

Genes skew the balance a bit but they don't write the whole story. I hated sport at school so I never did any athletics or games that would have helped me develop strength and power. Then, all my adult life, I've tried to keep up my running whenever possible, so I'm trained for keeping going. My slow muscle fibres have developed to the full, and what little fast potential I ever had has been pretty much ignored.

As we approach a set of chicanes in the track, where a minor road crosses the cycleway, I can see the familiar white and orange of our van in a tiny lay-by.

'Oh. Mandy. Didn't expect you.'

'Thought I'd try and catch you. How's it going? You look a bit limpy.'

'Just stiff in the back, need to do something.'

I don't really want to stop but I reckon it might settle things down a bit. A few minutes of pigeon-pose and figure-of-fours usually helps. I find a patch of grass and scan for dog shit. The ground is a bit rough but I manage the stretches alright and the investment is worth it. Soon Jenny and I carry on.

On the left there are occasional gaps in the trees and views over the Derwent Valley. I'm surprised how far we can see and how elevated we are. This is a beautiful leafy line through the countryside, sandwiched between industrial relics and urban modernity. And it doesn't really matter if I'm pretty sore now. The miles are ticking by. I feel like I'm getting slower but Jenny says not. In any case, it doesn't matter, as long as I just keep going.

One of the main ways muscles adapt to keeping going is by increasing the numbers of tiny energy-generating machines within them called mitochondria. Mitochondria are mind-blowing. They are little beings within beings. Back in our ancient evolutionary past, when our ancestors were single-celled microbes, they engulfed other creatures which could do the biochemical trick of turning chemicals into energy. Some of these 'engulfed others' became mitochondria, and they have DNA of their own, which isn't anything to do with the DNA inside our 23 chromosomes.

Out of the 20,000 or so genes I have inherited, only a handful of them are inside my mitochondrial DNA but these genes are special because of the unique way they are handed down. Nobody gets mitochondria from their dad. Like every other person, boys included, my mitochondrial DNA comes only from my mam. And it came from her mam, and her mam and so on. None of this has anything at all to do with any male ancestor. This portion of my DNA has been passed down through the female line only—a matriarchal thread, a gift from all the grandmothers I've ever had. I know precisely nothing about my great-grandmother Mary, who was Jack's wife. And I wonder what really happened to her daughter Maggie, the woman Muriel referred to as her 'real mam'? Did she die only of TB as was written in the official records, or did she die of neglect and relentless domestic abuse? I'm told by a relative that her life with Bob Robson was so horrible that she 'gave up living'.

One thing I know for certain is that Muriel loved her mother dearly but she swept her grief under the carpet; she told us her stepmother was our 'nanna' and rarely mentioned her 'real mam'. Maggie's untimely death was the pivotal event in my mam's life;

and because so much depends upon our mothers, it was also an important influence on mine. If Maggie had survived, there would have been an unbroken strand of love in our family. Maggie Nowell—how could you abandon my mam like that when she was only eleven? (There I go, indulging in my culture's habit of blaming the victim, blaming the woman.) But you were needed, with your piano-playing hands and your books of pressed flowers and your smile. Those who depart from this world without finishing their work leave unfillable holes. There is a strand of your DNA inside my cells which is purely you, Maggie. The little part that's women only, in the mitochondria, and not in the chromosomes that got mingled with that tyrant Bob Robson. The longer I run, the more the mitochondria in my muscles replicate. Making more mitochondria is a key way in which muscles become endurance trained. I should be grateful, my dear grandmother, for what you did give me; but I'd rather have met you than have to just imagine you.

At least Jack was spared the grief of his daughter Maggie's death. In 1925, when Jack was 51, his wife Mary died, followed in 1928 by Charlie his only son, who was 21. Jack died in 1933, at age 59 and Maggie, his firstborn, died in 1936. Mary, Maggie, Charlie and Jack—all their deaths are attributed to tuberculosis. Which was not remarkable because this little bacterium had killed a quarter of the adult population of Western Europe in the nineteenth century; and it was still thriving in the first half of the twentieth, especially in the working-class north of England where fresh air, fresh food and freedom from the terrible conditions of the chemical works, mines and shipyards were rare. 'Tuberculosis' is on their death certificates but these documents don't tell the stories of all the things that killed them. And yet Jack's running club, the Gateshead Harriers, went from strength to strength, and keeps on going.

At Rowlands Gill we leave the railway line and run along a road again, past a garage, and then follow the signs back to the line. It's striking how, within a very short distance, a busy traffic pulsed road can fade into the background when back on the line protected by the trees. The trees are doing their best to save us from ourselves. I think they're in my tribe. There are some trees living in our valley in Cumbria that are almost two millennia old. I go to them sometimes just to be in their presence. It is a kind of worship, although I am an atheist.

My back pain has eased a bit, probably because I know we are very close now, although it's hard to get a sense of distance as I have been trundling along the mostly tree-protected old line all morning. It can take years to train endurance muscles to increase their mitochondria but it's these mother-carried little engines that give my muscles the power to run. The mitochondria themselves are vital; although the DNA carried inside the mitochondria probably doesn't account for much of the variation in different people's running ability because there are only a few genes contained in it and because there is only a limited amount of diversity within its code.

It's unlikely that my mitochondrial genetics is boosting my stamina by much; but if it is, the advantage didn't come from Jack but from his lost-in-the-mists-of-time wife Mary and from her female lineage. Mitochondrial DNA is a historical tool which helps genealogists to trace human lineages. When DNA is passed on without being mixed up with other DNA, it's easier to trace its origins. I wonder if my many times great-grandmothers, whose uncombined mitochondrial DNA is living on within all my organs, were wise and respected elders who knew what it was to belong within the cycles of the Earth and the culture of their people? Or were they frightened slaves, whose bodies were not their own? My DNA cannot reveal these stories but still, in some ways, our bodies are history books, recording not just our own lives but life itself.

North of Rowlands Gill, we come to the Nine Arches Viaduct, another impressive structure, but this time with stone parapet walls and no suicide railings. There's a view over the river, way below our feet and out over the wooded valley. So many trees in the Derwent Valley. I had no idea. And we are looking out for the red kites who now live here in abundance, after their reintroduction over ten years ago. We don't see any kites but Jenny points out the ironically named Monument to British Liberty, which from this distance appears as a little phallus on a rolling hill. Taller than Nelson's column, it was commissioned by the aristocrat and coal baron George Bowes and erected in the 1750s as a testament to his wealth and his Whig politics.

The politics is difficult to decipher, but the liberalism it is said to represent seems to have more to do with keeping out the Catholic monarchs and protecting the interests of the British upper classes than social justice, as we would understand it. George Bowes was a 'Geordie' in that he supported the Hanoverian succession in the British monarchy. His monument stands on the Gibside Estate, which—by the time the railway came—had been inherited by the Earl of Strathmore, who would not allow the line to pass through the estate. Just as well—since at its busiest this line carried half a million passengers per year. Wouldn't want all those low-lives ogling at the gentry. It is the Earl's wife, Mary Bowes, who is more famous though, mainly because of her colourful private life and the fact that she became a pioneer by legally keeping her inheritance after divorcing her second husband. Celebrity culture is not new. Perhaps it was another export from the North-East.

On the sideboard of our house in Thorney Close Sunderland, out of my small reach, was the bear. About a foot in length and frozen in the act of walking forwards on all fours, with the left front leg outstretched. Her ceramic coat was a green glaze of many colours—iridescent when the sun or the filament light shone in our sitting room. When I think of the bear, it reminds me of the aurora borealis. I saw those lights once. It was when I was a teacher at Howtown Outdoor Centre, on the shore of Ullswater, and I had just spent the evening instructing my group of almost-teenagers how to orienteer in the dark. With maps and compasses and clad in standard-issue waterproofs, they ventured out in twos or threes to find their bearings under the whispering trees and searching owls. After an hour or more, my students straggled in like changelings, gleaming and exuding the cold excitement of the night. Then they drank hot chocolate and headed to their dorm for pillow fights and illicit late-night chit-chat.

Leaving them in the care of the teacher who had brought them from their own school, I headed out for last orders. But I never got my beer as I was waylaid by the surreal light show that was turning my familiar fells into something like the scene of an alien invasion. The Northern Lights. Green and shimmering. I stood immobilised and mesmerised. My body like a compass needle lining up under an immense cosmic magnetism. The sky danced brilliantly above the shining lake, then faded back to black. And I wondered why people ever needed to tell stories about stuff that did not actually happen when what *does* happen is things like this. Although that light show was altogether grander and far bigger than the green bear on my mother's sideboard, their colours matched exactly.

The bear came from Canada. It was a gift from my mother's stepmother, Nanna Robson. Her travels had been paid for by the compensation she got for having her leg crushed by a drunken driver on the seafront at Blackpool illuminations. I did not know Nanna Robson in her travelling days. I knew her when we visited her high-rise residence on Low Fell, Gateshead. I hated the musty lift, the tiny flat, the lack of anything to do and not being taken any notice of.

'Children should be seen and not heard,' was my mam's mantra whenever Nanna Robson was around.

Nanna never seemed to say much to me, and I never once saw her go out. Eventually she got dementia and visiting her in 'the home' made me sick with fear. And I could never really associate this distant dribbling shell of a woman with the shimmering bear, which she had brought from an exotic far-away place.

My mam told me that Nanna Robson had spent two years in hospital after being run over by the drunken driver, and Mam never missed visiting twice a week. But 'When the compensation came through, she didn't spare a penny. It all on went on the gallivanting.'

Except for the gift of the bear upon her return. The bear herself stood quietly in our house where she was completely different to any of the other inhabitants. The bear had things which none of us possessed. She was sleek and beautiful and had poise and style. She was classy. She also had special powers. The bear was a messenger from a big wide world of adventure, beckoning me into my imagination. And her green light seemed to glow out of her like a kind of magic. She was also a comforter and made me feel safe. Amongst all the fights and the chaos and the wounds, in her shimmery green coat with her left paw stretched out, she made me feel calm. The bear was the one who made me feel most confident about survival.

A few months after Muriel's death, I realised I couldn't remember what we had done with the bear when we cleared out her house. I rang my brother who sounded nonplussed and couldn't even remember it. I was sure he must have it, but he said not. I found myself looking on the internet for ceramic green bears and located a bear that looked exactly like ours, made in a pottery in

Canada. I thought it must be from the same family of bears, so I sent off some money and a few weeks later, very carefully wrapped in a big box, she arrived. She is on my bookshelf now. I take her for the same glowing guardian that was always on our sideboard. Not all stepmothers are wicked. I'm sure my mam's stepmother did her best. But she was no substitute for her 'real mam'.

I've had an ache in my left calf which is now becoming a pain and my foot is suddenly hurting every time it hits the ground. I stop.

Jenny looks concerned, 'You okay, Jules?'

'Dunno. Something wrong with my foot.'

I move to the side of the track and stretch my calf out on an old building stone with a rounded edge. I notice through the heavy shadows the outline of an old platform at about waist height. I sit down, take off my shoe to check for stones, and rub my foot. Jenny draws my attention back to where we are.

'Imagine all those people waiting here for the train. All the journeys and all the stories. It would have been bustling on that platform a hundred years ago. So quiet now.'

We just soak it in for a few moments. Jenny hands me some water.

'I'm okay to carry on now, Jenny.'

We run through some bollards and onto tarmac, past some new little houses, all in a neat row. My foot hurts but I can still run. Think I'll change my shoes when I get to the van.

Suddenly here is the van, and Mandy, and the River Tyne is less than a mile away. We are at the Blaydon Rugby Club and we can rest here for a while. Jenny gets out some homemade flapjack. I take off my shoes and check for blisters. Mandy makes tea and puts our camping chairs up in the car park. No harm in having a breather. And we need to message the Harriers and let them know our ETA.

The Hairy Fish

In these moments when your last heavy breaths
drawn from the syrup of hospital air
make false noises of a little more life,
I cannot change things.

I cannot alter the hate-love, violent disregard
between you, my little boy father
and the person who was your daughter.
I have my own version of good.

Can you know now, with dull eyes
and weak wilting heart
what you have never known?
For I have discovered something.

I have discovered something as good
as the hermit crabs and hairy fish
I dragged you across the rocks to stare at.
Shh now, I'll tell you.

The drowning girl you cast off
from your barren island is living
as if the idea that love can be trusted
—is true.

I sit here with you, waiting and
wanting to say that you mattered,
you made a mistake to think
we didn't care how you were.

There's more I can tell you,
yes—even as delicate and wild
and good as the hairy fish.
Shh now. Can you hear the shhh
of the sea?

13 *Time is of the Essence*

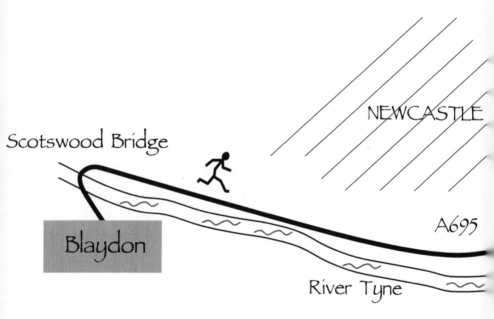

After a traumatic experience the human system of self-preservation seems to go onto permanent alert; as if the danger might return at any moment.

Judith Lewis Herman, Trauma and Recovery

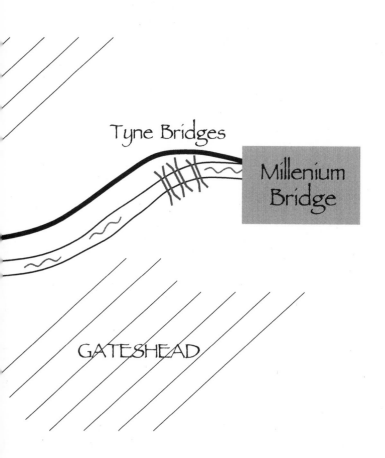

Running past warehouses and industrial yards, through snickets leading towards the river, the day is sultry and the air does not quench my thirst for breath but seems to choke me up. It isn't polluted, not with chemical outputs anyway, as it would have been in Jack's time, but the heat and humidity of the riverside and its associated memories are sending me into a trance of sadness. My legs feel heavy and it is becoming hard to keep running at all. Jenny cycles near me but stays quiet and lets me have my emotional space.

At the railway bridge she directs me over the stairs to the walkway, while she takes the longer cycle route. We go west for a short while, along the Keelman's Way, right next to the river. We say hardly anything. I am lost now—in my own old world. I have no idea if she can sense anything of what I am going through. Her job is just to be there if needed, to prevent me getting geographically lost. But she does know, I think, although we haven't talked about it, that she's giving me a lot more than that. Because something familiar and terrifying is happening to me. I'm struggling not to sit down on the kerb and weep. Because Jenny is here, I don't do that. Instead, I just keep plodding on at the same metronomic pace, not because I would be embarrassed to express my emotions in front of my friend but because to do so would be self-defeating. I will allow myself to feel sad inside—but I will keep running. I will not try to cheer myself up—but I will keep running. I don't understand why this feeling is almost overwhelming—but I will keep running.

Approaching the Scotswood Bridge, I tell myself to concentrate. I was a little worried when we planned the route, because running across a bridge carrying a major dual carriageway sounded a bit hazardous for someone like me, who is more used to running on moor and fell. Jenny assured me it would be fine and so it was. There's a pedestrian pavement all the way. The river underneath is slow and wide, and I can see all the famous Tyne bridges downstream to my right. Newcastle and Gateshead are two halves of a marriage, connected by these iconic structures.

We turn eastwards again, along the north bank of the Tyne, along a grey tarmac cycleway a couple of yards wide, with fields and scrublands on our left and a hedge on the right separating us from the main road and the river. Every footstep becomes not just a following-on but a conscious choice; not an act of escaping from my fears but of facing up to them. To put me on a psychologist's couch and get me to face these emotions would be an act of torture. But if I let the sadness exist while I'm running, it becomes possible to process things, bodily. I'm frightened. I begin to wonder if this whole thing was a huge mistake. Instead of being an affirmation of my roots, is it turning into a painful and unnecessary dredging up of things long buried?

At this moment all I can think about is my dad. There is a tiny voice inside me that only just stops me having a meltdown. 'These are only memories. Things that exist inside yourself. Of all the things to be frightened of in this world, you don't need to be frightened of yourself.' I hang onto that quiet inner wisdom. It's not that I can fully trust it but, in this moment, I make a really big effort to suspend my disbelief. I'll try and go with that voice for now. I'll try and just let myself feel but not be afraid of the feelings. I'll try and keep running. The fact that I am nearly at the end of the run feels irrelevant. To feel what I feel and to calmly keep running. Each footstep is a long way.

It was Friday afternoon, payday at the shipyard, and it was my dad's job to put the pounds and pence into small brown envelopes, according to the timesheets, and to mark it down correctly. Then he would stand at the door of the prefabricated office as each worker came to collect his wages. R.B. Harrison's wasn't a big shipyard but it was one of the last on the south side of Tyne—the workforce measured in dozens rather than hundreds.

The office was a shack just inside the gates of the yard on a rough track leading down towards the water. Inside the office was a creaky plyboard floor and large desks in each corner. My dad's desk was on the left as you went through the door. The place was shabby and spacious, and even on bright days the light was subdued. To a little girl, the dim atmosphere made it seem that exploring the other side of the office was an adventure.

Dad didn't give clear instructions about how to behave when I went in but there was an obvious expectation that I would be quiet and almost unseen. I have racked my brain for a logical reason as to why I have these memories of Friday afternoons, but I cannot make any sense of why I was there. If we were on our way to the caravan at Amble for a holiday or a weekend, I would usually get the bus and train after school and meet Dad at Newcastle Central Station. The only theory I can come up with is that perhaps my mam gave me a lift on the back of her moped to his work, and I then got the bus to Amble with Dad and she carried on alone, on the bike.

My confusion about the scenario is a reminder that memory is not a record of events, but a record of emotions tagged together with some snippets of external details. I thought it was good that my dad seemed to have an important role, to be in charge of the cash. But

I didn't like the way he behaved in the office. He was subdued, and subordinate to the other occupants. One day I almost breached the hierarchy disastrously. There was a door in the centre of the wall at the other end of the office and I was curious about what was behind it, so I sneaked over there, trying not to creak the floor, and reached for the handle as my dad, who darted with uncharacteristic speed behind me, grasped my arm.

'Don't you dare open that door. That's the boss's office. You'll get us the sack.'

I didn't know what he meant by 'the sack'. Sack of what? But all I needed to know was that I should sit in my dad's corner quietly and not move from there and I should say nothing until it was time to go. The fact that there were people in the world who my dad was obviously scared of was unsettling. This was a different order of things. At home he was *the Boss*. He controlled how much house-keeping money Mam was allowed, when we could have the lights on, and when and what we could watch on the telly. Our house-hold was the embodiment of what British Conservative politicians approvingly described as 'family values'. Society may steal a man's creativity by putting him to repetitive work, so that his mind is deadened, and the state may steal his time and health by setting economic policies which keep his wage packets from getting too full. But to quote my mam, 'It's a well-known fact' that in his own home a man 'should wear the trousers'.

As the men came to the shipyard office door for their wage packets, Dad said it was okay to speak to them, but they would be mucky, so I wasn't to touch them. It was okay to speak to those lower down the pecking order but not those above. This was my Friday afternoon lesson and, as an excellent student, I took it all in.

Newcastle announces itself along the Scotswood Road in the form of huge box-like, modern, industrial warehouses and car dealerships. I feel bewildered, entranced and unsure of what is real and what is imagined. Past and present and future no longer seem to occupy a timeline paced out in units. My perception of time has already been altered by the experience of lockdown. We joke with neighbours that, if you have more than two commitments in a week, life suddenly starts to seem busy. March was unseasonably warm. As we were locked in, plants and animals came out. April, and May running into June, have been lived in a kind of suspended animation, and I wonder if time, or anything else, will ever go back to ticking along like it used to, when the pandemic is over.

My blood runs cold when I think what it would have been like to endure a lockdown in a house with my parents. We would have been at more risk from each other than the virus. In the rhythm of my run on this hot autumn morning, my childhood feels as long ago as the primordial soup, while also feeling like it is happening now. As I'm running, I can feel my own past all wrapped up within me; and each breath, each step, is not a separate act but simply a running on of something which started long before I did. My pace is still metronomic. I begin to appreciate time—not as a quantifiable commodity, to be spent or wasted or saved—but as the unreliable narrator of our stories.

Each cell in my body has a way of telling the time, just like the barnacles, beloved by both Mr Darwin and me. We have clocks inside us which give us a sense of the Earth's rhythm. Even if we are locked up for weeks in the dark, our body clocks will still keep time. Human circadian clocks seem to be set at a little bit longer than twenty-four hours but they keep getting corrected by the real world of night and day and external clocks. Our bodies wait for the world to keep us in our rhythm, but if there's no night and day, we have an inbuilt mechanism telling us when to be active and when to rest. Resting is not just less activity; it's a change of metabolism and cellular chemistry, alteration of hormone levels and the switching off and on of different genes. Resting is the quiet movement in the symphony of our day. But quiet music is no less complex to orchestrate. My body is a kind of time machine that is constantly correlating to external reality. But here I am, strung out between the past and the now. It's my feet on the ground, the left foot, right foot, left then right. It's the turn of Jenny's bike wheels. It's the red-and-white vest covering my beating heart. These are now, these are real. I'm trying to hang onto them and not succumb to the illusion that the past has returned. It's only memories, only what's inside. I'm telling myself, 'Don't be afraid of the past, it's really gone.'

I'm realising that time is just as difficult as geographical space to navigate. I have a running friend who can tell me, almost to the minute, how long we've been running, even when we have been out for hours and she's not wearing a watch. I usually have no idea and hugely underestimate; I can run for an hour and think it was only 45 minutes. Yet now, on this pilgrimage, I feel like I've been running for years, actually for an unmeasurably long time, as if the run has no beginning and no end.

There's a saying, usually attributed to the master of time, Albert Einstein: 'The only reason for time is so that everything doesn't happen at once.' But I have this odd perception now, as my feet go forward in turn—over and over and over—that everything *is* happening at once. As if all the things that have ever happened are somehow present now, in this air, this breath, these legs running along this riverside.

The north bank of the Tyne seems never-ending and I know the thick tar of emotion I am running through is all wrapped up with Dad. It was the river. The way the low tide unveiled the mudbanks, upstream of Scotswood. The river looks just like it did when I used to visit Dad in his office; and I can feel his presence, this sad aggressive man, reawakened in my imagination. He was not stupid or humourless or lacking in kindness at times, but he was brutal. What made him rape his wife instead of charming her? Once a distant cousin told me a story about how my dad came to be living with his grandmother when he was a boy. After being locked in his mother's house upstairs for days, after being beaten by his step-father, Dad ended up escaping. The details were sketchy, and I was less than ten when I was told this story and trying to close my ears. And I've tended to take the hard line that a bad upbringing is no excuse for bad behaviour. I get that he was not nurtured, and he was probably traumatised and struggling. But he had choices, didn't he?

And I think about Mam's dad, the cocky apprentice barber Bob Robson, who was by all accounts pretty suave when he came to court my grandmother, but after they had wed became the tyrant head-of-household who regularly claimed his conjugal rights. So much so that I was told, by another distant relative, that Maggie Robson endured several back-street abortions, forced on her by the husband who refused to support a large family but still wanted his wife to give him his dues.

What turned these men into tyrants when they crossed their own front steps? Was it traumas from their own difficult beginnings or had they simply inherited a set of values in which a man was 'the lord of the house'? This toxic version of masculinity does not simply come from bad parenting but from a societal inheritance. For generations, the English aristocracy have emasculated the common man by stealing his property and making him work like a slave while they ride about hunting and living it up. We have inherited a hierarchy and, if a man must subordinate himself to his superiors, then at least he still has his household to obey him. As my legs run on, my thoughts also run away with me. All this psychologising is academic. What motivates one person is different from the next, and different from one week to the next. Generalisations are dangerous. Mostly, we all just get into ways of being; and the hardest thing of all is to change the habits we have evolved.

I want to change the sadness and shame that I carry around inside me by association with these men. The poisonous notions they have passed on are not in my genes but in my beliefs, my memories, my stories. I can disown them. Just disown them—why is this not easy? With my mam I shared some fleeting moments of love, just enough, and I held her hand when she died and brought her ashes home for my brother and I to scatter in a special place. I held my dad's death-bed hand too, after not seeing him for years. It was a duty. He had nobody else. I didn't go to the funeral. I tried to forget him. Now I'm caught in vicious conflict. I want to say I never loved him but that would be a downright lie. No matter how much I want it to be true, it would be a post-truth airbrushing to say I have no love for my dad. But where can my love for this detestable man live? Where can I put it, what am I meant to do with it? The fact that I'm even thinking about him makes me angry.

It was John who came up with the idea of crossing the Tyne and running along the north bank of river when we studied my options on the map. He realised it would be better than navigating through complicated streets to the south. In the planning I didn't think about any association with my dad at all, but now I feel this physical pain in my heart and I can't join up a single sensible thought. I want to cry, so much. I don't say anything to Jenny and don't make eye contact. I tell myself I can keep calm. On the verge of disintegration, I try to tell myself the feelings can be there and not overwhelm me. Just let it all be. Breathe, keep running, breathe, keep running, keep breathing, keep running. The tide is creeping upriver. The water is flowing up the mudbanks and lifting the silt from the riverbed. I will keep running. As the tide flows in and covers the mudbanks—I will keep running.

As we make our steady way towards Newcastle Quayside, I'm wrapped up in a world of painful nostalgia, not concentrating on my surroundings. Suddenly we seem to be right by the river and alongside the gleaming offices which are a testament to an outwardly levelled-up city. It's years since I've been here, and I'm impressed by how smart it all looks. What a beautiful city; am I dreaming? Then, in a second, I'm completely snapped out of my trance of sadness when the two Gateshead Harriers, who have been messaging me along the way, but who I have never met in person, appear in their red-and-white vests with big smiles.

Now the spell is broken. I'm running along the Newcastle Quayside in the sunshine with Richie Robbins on my left and Dave Leng on my right and we easily fall into stride with each other. My companions are concerned I might be tired but I'm not in the least. Running is easy. Jenny is hanging back on the bike. Dave and Richie and I talk and talk all the way to the Millennium Bridge. New old friends. I learn a bit about them, and they learn a bit about me, and nothing about this seems odd to them. They accept my wish to honour Jack Nowell, and to carry out this pilgrimage. They accept me and my story because they understand that, although before this afternoon we have only met via email, we are very much part of the same story. I'm not a Gateshead Harrier officially, but today I feel I am.

We run on past the railway bridge and the swing bridge and the famous Tyne Bridge. Just over the river is the beautifully named Bottle Bank, where Muriel and her sister Sheila would have dare-devil races on their bikes over the steep cobbles. The Sage Gateshead is a silvery curving edifice just across the river. I don't even know if Mam ever saw Gateshead after the Sage was built in 2004 in this shining 'City of Culture'. I know she saw the Millennium Bridge and she thought it was beautiful, but she'd say, 'It's all changed though since we were kids. Everything's changed. Yu wouldn't even recognise parts of Gateshead now.'

And now here I am on the Millennium Bridge, gathered up into the Gateshead Harriers' family. We cross the bridge but halfway over we stop, so Jenny can take a picture. I savour the moment. There's still a little way to go to the stadium but I've made it to Gateshead, my ancestral home. What a glorious, gorgeous place it is.

It was a late afternoon in April 1941 and only-just-eighteen-year-old Muriel was flying down Bottle Bank in Gateshead on her three-speed bike, her pride and joy which she'd paid for herself with her wages from her job in the milliner's shop. It was a job she hated. She feared the milliner—and the rats that infested the basement where she had to sort out the stock of hat-making materials.

As the lowliest employee in the shop, Muriel also had to make and serve the tea. The thing she hated most was having to steal an ounce or two per day, slipping it into a little twist of brown paper, at the behest of her stepmother. If she didn't come home with the tea there'd be trouble and she'd get less pocket money back from her wages. She was caught between the fear of her parents and the fear of losing her job. But now her working day was done and she had a few moments of freedom, whizzing down towards the Tyne, on her way to her short-hand and typing class, to get a qualification and a much better job. Soon she would be a short-hand typist, a profession she was proud of until her late twenties, until she got married and pregnant with my brother and, as women tended to do, gave up work. Then, after twenty years of de-skilling while she was confined to housework, she could only get a job packing for a mail-order firm. My dad begrudged her even that.

'I used to be a short-hand typist,' she would tell me in a tone reminiscent of an athlete proudly recalling their previous personal best but sad that they could no longer achieve it.

'I went to evening classes and my dad paid, but I had to pay him back. I was on me way there one time when the sirens went. Eee, I looked up and I saw the German planes coming up the Tyne. I saw them coming Julie, coming to bomb us, to flatten the place. I'll never forget it but the sirens were going and then I didn't dare look and I pedalled like mad and got home and into the shelter. I'll never forget it. Eee, it makes me feel sick to think about it. Everybody says the war years were good because folk pitched in together. But it wasn't good, pet. It was awful. Thank God you'll never have to go through anything like that, pet. That's all I can say.'

Manifesto

After Mary Oliver

You were speaking to me
weren't you Mary Oliver,
asking what it is I plan to do
with this one wild and precious life?

It's time you had an answer.
After all your diligent patience,
after all the times you never failed
to teach me how to fly.

This is what I plan to do—
to take another breath and speak
of unkept secrets hidden in plain sight
to swear an oath to the pink blushes
of stolen winter light.

I plan to speak the wildness
to give it form and words
I plan to drink the raindrops
to hear the unheard.

I plan to stare on mountaintops
climb high and face the sun
to burst with life, to scream out loud
to run and run and run.

I plan to know and tell it all
the wildest of the wild
and bear the gorgeous visions
then go out with the tide.

The soft-lipped kiss of death's farewell
—as air takes back our breath.
If I had not run for my life
would I have lived at all?

14 *Every Step*

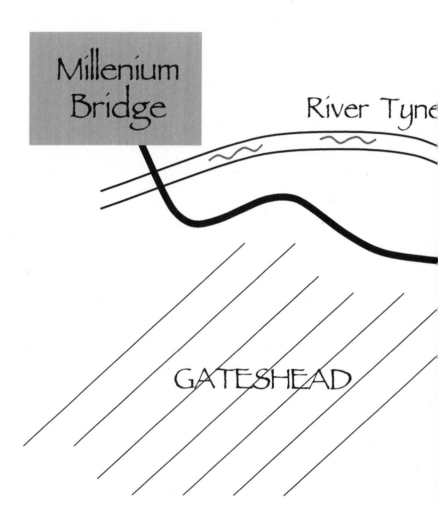

Millenium Bridge

River Tyne

GATESHEAD

Without community there is
no liberation.

Audre Lorde, Sister Outsider: Essays and Speeches

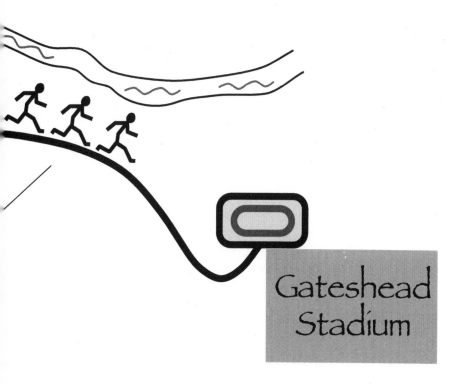

Gateshead
Stadium

On a muddy school playing field in Hebburn, near Gateshead, the local over-elevens boys' football team were losing two-nil with five minutes to go. It was 1956, and the only boy to believe his team could rescue the situation was the almost nine-year-old Brendan Foster, who was so good he had been promoted beyond his age. Foster made a run down the wing, dribbled past two defenders, and chipped the ball to his teammate to strike. The ball sailed wide of the mark, to the disappointed sighs of Foster and his older teammates. No more goals were forthcoming before the final whistle.

Brendan was undeterred—even more determined to win next time. He had always loved playing football, and football in the North-East was a kind of religion. The boys' matches were usually on Saturday mornings, and in the afternoons Brendan would indulge in his second sport, running, and go to the Gateshead Harriers for a race. This pattern continued for a few years, into his grammar school days. In his junior school, only four or five kids had passed the 'eleven plus' so Brendan was already a relative rarity and was keen to make the best of himself. He always believed he was going to be good at something—he just didn't know exactly what.

Brendan was the oldest of five siblings in a loving family where his parents never drove him to excel. They encouraged him, and nurtured him, but there was no hint of pressure. The drive came from something innate within the boy himself.

One Saturday morning, he was ready in his football kit as usual, but when he got to the playing field the game was cancelled because the pitch was frozen and dangerous to play on. That afternoon he arrived at the Harriers fresh legged, for a three-mile race—his first win.

'So, I thought to myself, oh hello, this feels good,' he later remembered. 'I like the feeling of winning. And maybe it's better to run a race where I'm in control of how well I can do rather than depend on all the others in the team for the win. Maybe I should concentrate on running a bit more and football a bit less, and see what happens.'

This is what happened—the boy was a promising junior runner but in his university years he had setback after setback. The graft he put in was astonishing, but that's what people don't see: the grinding weeks and months and years of hard unglamorous work, training in the cold and dark and meantime getting on with life, passing a degree, qualifying as a teacher, having a demanding full-time job. And still training over a hundred miles a week come snow or sunshine. Brendan always thought he would be really good at something and, as time went on, he wanted that something to be running.

He was a good athlete at school and when he joined the Harriers as a boy he did well, but not exceptionally so. The genetically influenced physical talent was there, although he wasn't from a family who excelled in sport. In terms of improvement through training, Brendan witnessed many of his teammates training their hearts out without making huge gains in speed, while others did the same training and got faster and faster. While he was at university, Brendan began to fear that he was not destined to be an international champion. He had the desire, and some basic talent, but his potential seemed to be limited.

We all have an inherent limit to our potential. We can train till the cows come home but eventually we reach a ceiling which we find difficult to breach. What governs this is a complex mix of biomechanics and physical build, physiology and psychology. The genes we inherit, the epigenetic marks passed on by recent ancestors, how our environment affects our development, our belief systems and temperament; they all influence our baseline capabilities and the extent to which our performance will improve with training.

Some things can change, and some can't. I can't change the shape of my vertebrae, but I can influence how well my back functions even though it's sub-optimally bent. I'll never be as good at running, or any other sport, as if I would have been if my genes had not influenced the bones to grow like that. But there is not, and never will be, another version of me without the Scheuermann's disease but identical in every other way, to compare to. It's down to using what I have in the best way I can, which is the same for everyone. Discovering the difference between the fixed and the changeable is, in part, what the athlete's quest is about. How good can I be?

Brendan began to doubt himself when he trained hard but his body didn't reward him with the hoped-for improvements. Yet he didn't give up until he found and solved the problem that was holding him back. It was a lack of iron. Without iron, there is a lack of haemoglobin, the protein in red blood cells which carries oxygen from the lungs and through the bloodstream to the muscles and other tissues. Brendan had been like a motor with an artificial limiter restricting his oxygen delivery system. But if Brendan's mindset had been a little less committed, he might have given up serious running before finding out that he could, and would, respond to training if his body was properly nourished. And respond it did, in spectacular fashion. He went on to become an Olympic medallist, a Commonwealth Champion, a European Champion a World Cross Country Champion and a world record holder. Brendan's story bears out the theory that there are three main ingredients to sporting success—baseline talent, trainability and mindset.

When thinking about the genetics of running ability, we may focus on physiology and physique but these are, to some extent, the servants of mindset. There is a theory that athletes are athletes because they get a deep emotional satisfaction from performing and excelling and that this emotional, some might even say spiritual, reaction is partly genetic—to do with the biology and chemistry of our brains. Brendan was the only boy on the pitch who believed his team could win even though they were two-nil down, and this frustrated him: if only his teammates would show a bit more faith in themselves; a bit more desire to actually win. And Brendan stuck it out with running because he had an instinct that this was the thing he was destined to be good at. Brendan's definition of good is exceptionally good! His success was a combination of DNA and determination. To what extent the determination itself is genetic we do not know, but physiology and psychology are not separate processes. The lead of depression, the tingling thrill of competing to your limit and being willing to believe you can extend that limit; our DNA may influence the likelihood of experiencing these things but the real story of what makes them happen is complex. Within that complex mix I still give credence to an idea many scientists are becoming dubious about. Free will. And within that complex mix, for Brendan and for me, there were also the circumstances in which we started running—Jack Nowell, Gateshead Harriers, the Great North Run.

We are definitely on Gateshead soil now as we leave the bridge behind and run on. My Harrier guides are gentle and encouraging. 'There's a bit of uphill before we get to the stadium but it's not bad. We'll take it steady.'

Dave and Richie have helped many a runner achieve their ambitions, accompanying them on the Great North Run and other races. They are both very involved with the club, encouraging members of all abilities, and they have that altruistic way about them—making me feel like they are there just for me, and willing me on. Maybe I should be either exhausted or elated but I'm neither.

'I'm fine actually. I feel fine. I'm used to hills; it'll be fine.'

I just feel calm and quietly happy. And curious at what it will be like when we arrive. Suddenly a new voice comes from behind, with a Scottish accent. 'You can run but you can't hide!'

We turn to see Gordon Bell, the Chair of the Harriers, joining us on his bike.

'I was looking for you on the Quayside but must have missed you.'

'Well, I duuno how yu missed us, lad. Anyway, we've got her, she's here. Julie, this is Gordon.'

Gordon seems nothing like how I imagined. When I emailed him, I was keen to make a good impression and worried that, as the Chair, he might be a bit serious and officious. He was incredibly helpful though, and has gone to a lot of trouble for me today. But when I thank him, he humbly brushes it off with a warm and friendly laugh.

'Oh, it's fine, no trouble. It's great to see you. Well done. I'm gunna bike up to the stadium, I'll see you on the track.'

'Okay, bonnie lad,' replies Dave, as we run on to tackle the hill, which turns out to be a gentle rise. As the ground flattens Richie gives the final encouragement.

'Well done, you've done amazing. We're here now. You've made it! Round the edge of that car park and through the gates.'

On an August afternoon in 1974, Brendan could hardly hear himself think as he stood on the line on the newly laid Tartan Track at Gateshead Stadium. The ten thousand screaming fans were full of expectation. He was now working as the Sport and Recreation Officer of Gateshead Council and his first job was to organise the Gateshead Games and put the venue on the map. A few months earlier, Brendan had made a bold claim to back up his vision of Gateshead as a hub of athletics.

'If the track gets laid, I'll run a world record on it.'

In the middle of his illustrious international career he was busy organising other athletes to come and run at Gateshead Games. This was his first major task in his new job, after leaving his post as a chemistry teacher at his old grammar school. But when the day dawned it wasn't just the organisation he was worried about. He also had the small matter of a world record to address. He was already a world record holder over the two-mile distance, but here he was, on the brand-new state-of-the-art track, beginning to wonder if he really could keep the promise made in an off-guard moment after he'd had a drink at a civic reception. But 7 minutes and 35.1 seconds later he could not only breathe a sigh of relief but also take in a draught of joy. Big Bren wasn't just talk. The games were a brilliant success and his world record was a great inspiration to the home crowd. Throughout the rest of the decade, he was a northern and worldwide star.

A few months prior to the first Great North Run in 1981, Brendan had met up with his friend Chris Brasher, in the Lake District. Perhaps Brasher, an Olympic gold medallist in steeple-chase, was pursuing one of his, sadly never successful, attempts at the Bob Graham Round. Brasher and Foster were each curious about what the other was planning, wanting to sound each other out nonchalantly, without giving too much away. Brasher had the London Marathon up his sleeve. The Great North Run was, as it turned out, over twice as big.

A couple of years earlier, Brendan had been in New Zealand, running a race called 'Around the Bays'. It was the biggest race he'd ever seen. Impressed by the level of participation, and the fact that the country's prime minister had fired the starting gun, showing how important running was becoming in New Zealand, Brendan was inspired to try organising a public race back on Tyneside. He got together with four other Gateshead Harriers. They were thinking of calling the race the 'Geordie Five Thousand', aiming for five thousand participants; but worried they would not get that many, they called it the Great North Run.

The BBC Look North office in Newcastle was inundated with sack-loads of entries and every one was sorted by hand and replied to by post. One of those entry forms came from my sixth-form friend Linda. When Linda came into school after the race, wearing her T-shirt, all sparkly eyed and glowing with pride, I realised where my choices lay. The tight band of a hangover round my head, the dry mouth, the detached and languid feeling of a young body metabolising booze was a contrast to the life that oozed out of my friend. She struggled with a tough family, as I did, but she had chosen a different medicine.

It took me years to really contain my drinking, but running stopped me from drinking to destruction. Since my teenage years I had relied heavily on alcohol to cope. But gradually, over decades, the more I realised I was loved by Mandy and by my friends, and the more I found reward in other pursuits, the less I needed to drink. I was like one of those rats in a cage who—given a choice of water or a solution of morphine to drink—will choose the drug; but put them in a cage with playthings and sandpits and tunnels to explore, and they will choose the water. I'm not sure if addictions are always diseases in themselves or can sometimes be symptoms of other absences. Our genes can make us more susceptible to having our reward systems hijacked. But when there is a different kind of reward available, which is genuinely more satisfying, it's only natural to go for that instead. I'm not disciplined enough to just do things that are good for me because of some theoretical benefit—I need a tangible motive. It's no coincidence that ex-addicts are over-represented in long-distance running. Some people say running can also be an addiction and I'm sure it can. But for me it's part of the cure. There's a difference between an addiction that feeds a rat, and one that nourishes it.

When Jack Nowell founded the Gateshead Harriers in 1904, there were running clubs springing up all over the place. In the nineteenth century, running had gone from something done by so-called 'pedestrians', a type of human racehorse betted on by the rich, to something pursued by gentlemen themselves—'noble amateurs'. The athlete became a symbol of vigour and nobility and the founding of the modern Olympics in 1896 further popularised the trope of the gentleman amateur. Money was banned from athletics and the talented poor would struggle to the surface of a largely unfunded sport, while holding down demanding jobs.

The democratising process started in clubs that sprang up all over the country in the late nineteenth and early twentieth centuries. There were hot-beds of athletics in the South of England associated with the men from posh public schools and gradually these became more open to the common man. And as the twentieth century dawned, the North-East also became a hot-bed of athletics. Saltwell Harriers were the first club in Gateshead 1890, and there were many more in the region.

It's hard to pinpoint the things that lead to a particular zeitgeist, but I wonder if the Newcastle Town Moor was a factor in the idea of running for sport creeping into the consciousness of the Geordie people. The Town Moor is a huge swathe of common land which never fell prey to the land grabs of the Enclosure Acts. Less than a mile from the beating heart of the city centre, the Moor is bigger than Hyde Park and Hampstead Heath combined. It's a place where both horses and humans have raced for a very long time. Large summer fairs have been held there since medieval times; but by the late 1800s the Hoppings, as the summer fair was known, also included running races, pole leaping, triple jump, running jump, tug-of-war, bar vaulting, bicycle races and lots of competitions for children. These events were encouraged by the temperance movement, which aimed to direct the common man's aspirations away from drinking and betting on horses and towards an ideal of clean living and self-improvement.

I have long been suspicious of the 'endurance ethic'. The endurance athlete can represent a symbol of virtue; one who has shown fortitude, moral backbone, strength of character to keep going and wring the best physical effort out of themselves. But is this some kind of over-valuing of the work ethic for its own sake? Is automatically equating hard work with virtue part of the capitalist plot to fool folk into slaving away? Or worse still, is it some hangover from religious notions of sin and piety and penance? I love running for the bodily experience of it but I question my motives when it comes to external measures of my *achievements*.

Jack Nowell, whose dad was also a Gateshead barber, would have gone to the Hoppings. I can picture them there together; Jack being egged on by his dad to try every race on offer. And when he was a grown man earning a decent living, he made his own Hoppings in Saltwell Park for the local kids in the streets where he lived. A bit like Brendan, he brought running back to his tribe; but he only brought it 5 miles and not halfway round the world.

Although my great-grandad's club, Gateshead Harriers, used to meet at St Mary's Church, that wasn't because he or the club members were religious; just that they were allowed a place to meet there. There were no changing rooms or hot showers but there was plenty of enthusiasm. I can only speculate as to why the North-East became an epicentre for running and why these blokes, many of them racked by tuberculosis as Jack was, were motivated to run. As is true for runners nowadays, they would have had many different reasons to run but, whatever their motives, they were creating their own moments of freedom. And they had no idea that in the process they also helped to create mine and Brendan's and those of thousands of others.

All the races I've ever run, all the times I've laced up my trainers and just gone out, even on the days when I don't go out for a run, running still saves me. I'm not proud because of any deluded sense of superiority over anyone else and their traditions. But I am proud to come from all this north-eastern running heritage. Flat running is not my friend any more and I said I'd never do another road marathon, yet the Town Moor Marathon is tempting. Well, I guess I could think about it. Whatever I choose to do with my running in the future, I'll run until I can't run any more. It just can't be any other way.

'Well done, you've done amazing. We're here now. You've made it!'

I'm running between my new-found teammates, Dave and Richie, and as we enter the stadium, turning left onto the track, they insist I don't just stop but do a full lap. I'm tired and hot but I step up onto my toes a little as the jog turns into a run, my stride opens, and my cadence increases to run like a proper runner to the finish line where Gordon has placed the framed photograph of Jack Nowell from the office wall. Because of the virus we can't go indoors together, so he has brought my ancestor outside to meet me. I hadn't asked them to do this, but it's wonderful how Gordon and Dave and Richie seem to totally get why this means so much to me. I don't really have to explain myself that much, they just seem to get it.

Smiles, hugs, handshakes. Standing in the sunshine on the cinder-red track, I'm introduced to the Olympian Angela Gilmour, who was also Commonwealth gold medallist in the 4 x 400m relay in 1990. Greeting me in her crimson Gateshead Harriers' T-shirt, and with a huge welcoming smile, she's interested to hear about Jack Nowell.

Angela's main concern is the junior runners in the club. She explains how not all the kids' families have the money for the kit and the travel but they help them out when they can. She's worried about the juniors missing training over the last few months because it's not just the running they will be missing. We talk about hardship and opportunity and setback and Angela tells me she is still going from strength to strength, recovering from a cerebral haemorrhage which almost took her life and stopped her running. As the sun shines down on us, I'm soaking up being in her presence. Angela radiates warmth and positivity, at the same time as acknowledging the hardships. I have so many things I want to ask but I'm awash with thoughts and feelings. She tells me how she loved running, about the grief of not being able to run, but how it hasn't stopped her being involved with the club.

'It's all about the youngsters now. We just want to give them the opportunities we had.'

I'm listening intently but out the corner of my eye I'm also sneaking a peak at Jack Nowell's framed picture propped up on the track. Then I notice that someone else has arrived. The boy from Hebburn, Sir Brendan Foster, comes over to say hello, to shake my hand, to ask me about the story, where I've run from and why. I do my best to cobble it together but I don't know if makes sense and if he will get it, like Richie and Dave and Gordon. Or will he just think I'm weird, and daft? I need not have worried. Within two minutes, I am relaxed in the great man's presence and realise he genuinely is a really nice bloke. We talk easily and he is keen to hear my tale and to respond thoughtfully to my questions, and he questions me in return.

'Running is in everyone's genes,' says Brendan. 'Otherwise none of us would be here. We were never able to run faster than our prey but we could run for longer and wear them down. That stamina—we must all have some of that in us, as humans. Running is natural. We didn't evolve to kick balls about or whack them with sticks, but we evolved to run.'

'True,' I say, 'but what made you a world-class runner and the lad round the corner just an average club runner? Was it the determination, the belief, the positive psychology? Is that something innate? Is it mostly the mind that makes the difference between a good runner and a great runner?'

Brendan looks at me with a kind and open curiosity. 'Yes, probably, could be. But not every talented kid gets the opportunities, even if they have a positive outlook and a good work ethic. And does it really matter how well you do, if it's the best possible for you?'

Brendan grew up in a world where both sport and education were valued, but where notions of success never dominated the relationships—the family and friendship networks that were the bedrock from which everything grew. Brendan has always been competitive within sport, but he has not made a competition out of life. Between our reflections, Angela and Brendan start to reminisce.

'Can you remember so-and-so? What happened to him? Did he marry that lass he was always chasing?'

They'd mention a character's name and exchange knowing looks and laugh, as they sparked off each other's memories.

'Running wasn't just about competition; it was our lives,' says Brendan as he recalls stories of raucous journeys back from races, practical jokes, friendships cemented by a common purpose.

Many famous, successful Tynesiders end up leaving the North-East. Getting on in the world—making their way. A few of them return, belatedly appreciating this place, but many don't; and although Brendan has travelled widely, he has not transplanted himself anywhere else. It is not a lack of ambition that has kept him here, it is his rootedness in his relationships with people and place. To me, this kind of belonging seems rare. To Brendan, I guess it's just natural. Can someone so 'belonged' ever understand the yearnings of the 'un-belonged'?

Brendan and Gordon suggest I should get my photo taken in the lane where the Jamaican sprinter Asafa Powell turned in a 100m world record performance in 9.77 seconds right here in 2006.

'It was lane four. Lane four, Julie—right here,' says Brendan.

I have to ask them how a sprinter lines up their posture in the blocks. I've never once raced on a track and to say I look less than convincing crouching in Powell's Lane is an understatement. But Brendan is full of nostalgic excitement, standing on this track. All the events he has lived out here are part of him and part of his legacy.

Whatever we think we might have achieved, it's almost certain to be perceived differently when we are dead and gone. The great forces of empire and industrialism, the ethic of commercial growth at all costs—the pioneers of these may have genuinely thought they were contributing a positive legacy. Now I wonder how the sport of running will be perceived by future generations. Will it be seen as an ego-driven bid by individuals to make their mark, and by countries to prove their greatness, an assertion of outdated tribal mentalities? Or maybe a commercially driven exploit, a fad to sell kit and charge a huge amount of money for race fees and prop up an industry of fitness trainers and physios? Will we still have a Great North Run in another forty years and, if so, what will it look like?

I quiz Brendan about the Great North Run and try to explain why it has been so important in my own story.

'Life wasn't very good when I grew up in Sunderland but my friend in sixth form ran the first GRN and got me running regularly. It kind of saved me really.'

'What do you mean, not very good.'

For a moment I was a bit disarmed by his directness.

'Well, you know, parents not coping, and alcohol, and violence, not good. And I'd already started drinking a lot by sixteen. Running was the only thing that helped.'

'Do you think it is in the genes then?'

'What, the running?'

'No, the drinking. It's not something to be ashamed of—some people would say it's a disease, isn't it?'

I hadn't expected the conversation to go like this.

'Yeah, but I was only a kid—and I was ashamed then. And I've carried the feeling with me. But I hope the drinking isn't in the genes. Even it is, that doesn't mean I have to be an addict. I have some choices, don't you think?'

'You know when we started the Great North Run, we had this ethos, we still have it, that running is good for people and should be encouraged. And so, we decided we ought to put on an event that provides a worthy stage for the people to run. Because every one of over a million people who have finished that race have a story. They have put themselves into it. They are the central character in their own plot, and what stories they have and what they make of it, we—as race organisers—have no control over that. We didn't know running was good for mental health. People started telling us it was, after they had done the races. We didn't invent what the race has become, the participants have invented it. It's down to them. It's down to people like you. Funny to think of it. That your great-grandfather invented the Gateshead Harriers; then us five Harriers put on the run, and you and your friend ran it like that. It's a thread of story itself.'

'I'm thinking of writing a book about it.'

I feel small and slightly bonkers, like this great hero might be interested or take me seriously. But he seems to, and he's given freely of his time and really listened to me and understood my story. I didn't expect that. Maybe if he had just come and shaken my hand, I would have been more than satisfied. I didn't expect him to give a lecture on how we all have a running heritage and how we all have stories and how I don't need to feel ashamed of my past. In the end I begin to feel guilty because he goes on, and seems not to be in a hurry. He might be Sir Brendan and have a busy demanding life but he has time for me.

'The thing about the Great North Run is that it has to be big. If fifty thousand people go to St James's Park to see the football, then we need at least that number in the race; otherwise we haven't changed anything, we haven't created a shift. A million finishers aren't even just a million stories because if a mother runs the race, then it also affects her kids, for the better. Everyone is central to their own story, but they are not the only character in it.'

'How do you see it changing in future? Do you worry that people are getting less active and less fit? The evidence, especially about the widening inequalities, isn't good.'

'Running is good for you and should be encouraged. And it's our job to honour that. I don't know what the hundredth Great North Run will look like, but I want there to *be* one. We have to stay true to the basic ethos and we can't dictate what people will make of it. We don't know what will happen, but something has happened in every race for forty years, except this year we can't run it and people had to do it individually. There's a big difference in sport between being a spectator and a participant. When you think about it, it's a kind of democracy. Participating changes you. Not everyone can be a champion, but most people can participate. And we were just a group of runners who started this run because we thought it would encourage people. We didn't know what would happen. We just knew something would happen. Then it evolved, and especially the mental health benefits—that was a kind of side effect we hadn't really thought about. Nobody talked about mental health much then anyway. We just knew that running felt good. It's very basic really.'

I can't imagine that organising something of the magnitude and magnificence of the Great North Run is basic. The vision may in some ways have been basic, but the reality is enormous.

'Yeah, but thanks for everything, Brendan. For helping me survive. I guess I'm a kind of side effect.'

'I suppose you are, Julie. But listen, well done and good luck with the book. I think it'll be good; you should definitely write it.'

I shrug; we laugh; we say goodbye. I feel good. I feel accepted— not because I'm someone special by dint of Jack Nowell being my great-grandfather but because I'm a runner with a story. To be told by someone who has achieved greatness in running that everyone's story is important, and that participation in running is a living enactment of democracy, and that these aren't just words. I'm proud to be Jack's descendant and to be from the North-East and to have had this time with Brendan and Angela and the Harriers. But this whole thing is not about pride. It started as a search for connection and belonging, and I did find those. But as wonderful as the connections I have made through this journey are, they are not as important as the sense of reconnection with myself.

Brendan has reminded me that we can live by a set of values which can influence our destiny but there is no destination, only participation. And a single life, the thing I call *me*, also evolves. I'm not the same as I was. Personal identity is also to some extent fluid. But there is one thing which can never change. I am a runner. Nobody can ever make me not a runner. When I was lying stock still inside the barrel of an MRI scanner with a broken body after the climbing accident, not knowing what the future would hold, I visualised myself running. I went through my lakeshore run at home in my imagination. After five minutes or so, I started sweating and my skin turned pink, even though it was cold inside the machine. Whatever happens to me, running has changed me and I can't be changed back.

The highest honour for me today has been meeting the Gateshead Harrier and former international running star Angela Gilmour. Even though she cannot physically run any more, she is still all about running and all about Gateshead Harriers. I won't forget that afternoon on the track. Angela can't choose to run any more, but she chooses not to leave it behind. I don't think Brendan runs any more, but he is the Geordie embodiment of running. The moment when he experienced the sense of control of his own destiny, which that first race win gave him, was pivotal. There *are* things we can control. With intelligence and hard work and hope— there are things we can control. The North-East is often portrayed as a heart-sink kind of place which has lost its prosperity. The poisonous politics that talks of 'levelling up', but enacts the opposite, is bankrupt. Opportunities, where they exist, come from our communities. From people like the Gateshead Harriers— Richie Robbins and Dave Leng and Angela Gilmour and Sir Brendan and Jack Nowell. Unlike Brendan, Jack was never a brilliant runner. But Jack loved running and he started something—and it evolved. And evolution, by definition, is not predetermined. It is driven, not by abstract ideology, but by the needs of our bodies and our souls. To run. To be together. To survive.

On a freezing January morning in Sunderland, I get out of my single bed with its Winceyette sheets and candlewick bedspread, the one with the monsters underneath it, and go downstairs in my running kit.

'Du yu want Cornflakes or Rice Crispies, pet? Eee, yu never going for a run in that weather, our Julie. You'll catch a death-a-cold. And mind, the path's dead icy, pet. I nearly measured me length coming back from the shops wi' the milk.'

'I'll be alrite, Mam. As long as I can go for a run, I'll be alrite.'

I open the door of 162 Tilbury Road and tread carefully on the icy path to the front gate three metres away. I squeeze the latch and my skin tingles on the cold metal. I shut the gate behind me so the street dogs don't get in and shit in Mam's rose bed. I turn left. The silent concrete road between the wide pavements has been gritted so I venture to the middle and break into a run.

At the edge of our estate the snow has been cleared and I run down Durham Road bank. The sun is coming out and everything is starting to thaw. There's not much traffic but the pelican crossing does that magical thing of lighting up the green man, even though there's nobody nearby to press the button. I run straight over and keep running. I keep on running; every step takes me closer. This moment is eternal. Every step I'll ever run—is a coming home.

Bibliography

Carey, Nessa. *The Epigenetics Revolution*. Icon Books 2012.

Darwin, Charles. *The Descent of Man*. Wordsworth Editions. 2013.

Darwin, Charles. *On The Origin of Species*. The Natural History Museum. 2019.

Epstein, David. *The Sports Gene*. Yellow Jersey Press. 2013.

Foster, Sir Brendan + Temple, Cliff. *Brendan Foster*. Heinemann. 1978.

Hari, Johann. *Lost Connections, Uncovering the real causes of depression – and the unexpected solutions*. Bloomsbury. 2018.

Herman, Judith. *Trauma and Recovery*. Basic Books. 2015.

Lewis, Richard. *The Great North Run – The first 25 years*. Kensington West Productions Ltd and Nova International Ltd. 2005.

Long, Stan + Merril Andrew. *From Dirt Track to Glory*. Gateshead Harriers. 1976.

Mehl-Madrona, Lewis. *Coyote Medicine*. Fireside. 1998.

Rutherford, Adam. *A Brief History of Everyone Who Ever Lived*. Weidenfeld and Nicolson. 2016.

Van Der Kolk, Bessel. *The Body Keeps the Score*. Penguin. 2015.

Wainwright, Alfred. *A Pennine Journey*. The Wainwright Society. 2019.

Watson, Jo. *Drop the Disorder, Challenging the Culture of Psychiatric Diagnosis*. PCCS Books. 2019.

Zimmer, Carl. *She Has Her Mother's Laugh, The Powers, Perversions and Potential of Heredity*. Picador. 2018.

Acknowledgements

I would like to express heartfelt and particular thanks to:

My wife **Mandy Glanvill**. For never wavering and keeping on sharing the journey with me. For loving me and supporting me in body, mind and spirit.

My editor **Kelly Davis**. For being brilliant, insightful, compassionate, accurate and dependable. Kelly is also a wonderful poet and author- see www.kellydavis.co.uk.

Richie Robbins and **Dave Leng** of Gateshead Harriers. For sharing the last couple of miles of my run and taking me into the fold when I arrived in Gateshead. And to Richie for continuing the friendship and helping me in so many ways.

Angela Gilmore, Gateshead Harriers first female international runner, Olympian and Commonwealth gold medallist. For meeting me at Gateshead Stadium with a huge smile. For giving your time and sharing your insights and stories and for reading the book pre-publication.

Sir Brendan Foster. For saving my life as a "side effect" of the starting the Great North Run. For taking the time to listen to me and answer my questions with wisdom and compassion.

Gordon Bell, Chairman of Gateshead Harriers. For making the whole thing possible.

Jenny Power, my longtime friend from Wylam. For supporting me on the last day of the run on her bike and for the flapjacks and the love.

Nichola Merrit. For running with me over Gowbarrow, and sharing our stories and friendship.

John Byrne. For saving my life from the cow, and for all the other savings of me. And for sharing his birthday with me on Westernhope Moor.

Vincent Booth, artist and runner. For the wonderful cover oil painting from a photograph taken by Jenny Power.

Kim and Sinclair Macleod, and Rachel Hessin of Indie Authors World. For cover and internal design, typesetting, and publishing support. And for their patience, expertise and friendly encouragement with all aspects of this book.

About the Author

Julie Carter grew up in Sunderland and lives near Keswick in Cumbria, UK. She started her working life as a researcher in genetics before teaching science and outdoor education then becoming a medical doctor. After a couple of decades working in emergency care and general practice, she began to look more broadly for different ways of promoting health  and alleviating distress. This led her to train in Human Givens which is an evidence-based practical approach to health based on getting our needs met in balance, without exploiting others.

Julie is a runner, a climber and an adventurer. Her experiences in all aspects of her life are the inspiration for her writing which crosses the genres of creative non-fiction and poetry. Her first book *Running the Red Line* was a five-star finalist in the Wishing Shelf Independent Book Awards and her second, *Is It Serious?*, is a collection of poetry on the subjects of family, love, science, medicine and wild things. Julie enjoys forming collaborations, making connections and speaking at events and festivals. Her film *I Am a Fellrunner*, co-directed by Jessie Leong, has won international praise and gained laurels in nine film festivals. She is currently working on her theatre production, *The Dreamtime Fellrunner*, supported by the Arts Council England.

You can find a selection of Julie's work including film and audio on her website www.mindfell.co.uk where you can also read her blog and see details of upcoming events including wild writing workshops and outdoor poetry events.

Also head to www.mindfell.co.uk to enjoy a selection of photographs to compliment this book.